THE
Honorable State
OF
𝔐𝔞𝔱𝔯𝔦𝔪𝔬𝔫𝔶
MADE
COMFORTABLE
OR AN
ANTIDOTE
Against
DISCORD
Between
MAN and *WIFE*
BEING
Special Directions for the Procuring
and Preserving of Family Peace

LONDON,
Printed for *Francis Pearse* at the *Blew-Anchor* at the West end of
St. Pauls. 1685

An Antidote Against Discord Between Man and Wife
Copyright © 2013 by Edification Press
All rights reserved

Edification Press
Culpeper, VA
www.edificationpress.com

This edition is based on the text of *The Honourable State of Matrimony Made Comfortable or An Antidote Against Discord Betwixt Man and Wife* published in 1685. The text has been minimally revised to reflect modern spelling. The original author of the treatise is unknown, but D.B. was cited to follow the conventional practice.

ISBN 978-1-936473-03-8

TO THE READER

Christian Reader,

The *Author* of this following Discourse (observing the hot contests that are too frequently between the nearest Relations, yea, between such as profess Relation to Christ; and observing the strange effects of their dissentions influencing them to do such things as tend greatly to dishonor God,) was very much pressed in his spirit to seek out some *Antidotes* that were proper to cure the fiery Distempers of their Spirits, that they might cease affronting God by their furious actings: And indeed God hath directed him to very proper methods for the accomplishing thereof, if those choleric Relations would condescend to make use of the Physic here prescribed. I never heard of any Treatise that was wholly on this subject before. I am confident there was never a Discourse of this nature in this method; none adventuring to deal so particularly and fully with such passionate Relations as he hath done. The great reason that it is so difficult to make up breaches between Men and their Wives is, because they are all averse to the acknowledging of their faultiness; every one conceits him or her self to be wronged. Therefore this Author hath endeavored to discover which of those Relations is most in fault when Discord doth arise between them, and that so the most faulty may be convinced thereof, and thereby influenced to a faithful endeavor of reformation. These *Antidotes* are not only proper to cure, but also to prevent Discord between such near Relations: So it will be of general use to all married persons. I could heartily wish that every professing Family had one of these little *Books*, there being in the *Appendix* laid down special directions for the right ordering of Family-concerns both in relation to Children and Servants, as a special means to preserve the peace of Families. O you Husbands and Wives that have felt the smart of your furious contentions, be willing to use the means to make your lives more comfortable. In this *Book* you will find helps by the blessing of God to enable you to take more complacence in each other, and to live more peaceably and lovingly together. Be not distasted with the Author for demonstrating the evil of your passionate wranglings for every trifle. Do not any of you lavish out reviling speeches against him, because by his characters you appear most faulty when there is Discord between you and your conjugal Relation. What the Author hath done in this respect, is wholly designed to put a stop to your dissentions, and to help you to live more peaceably and sweetly together; And if you would seriously peruse the *Book*, you would find it so. I need not enlarge in the commendation of the *Book*. When once you have read the *Book*, you will see cause to commend it yourselves, and to thank the Author for the pains he hath taken therein to so good an end. *Reader*, that thou may'st by the perusal of this *Book* be helped to a more peaceable living with thy conjugal Relation, is my hearty prayer: *Farewell.*

D. B.

THE
PREFACE

The Author of this following Discourse hath ventured farther than any that I have yet met with that have gone before him. It is dangerous interposing in the differences between Man and Wife, lest both fall foul upon him for his fair endeavors: the Man being ready to be over-careful of his Free-hold Tenure, the Woman of her Copy-hold; and 'tis a venturous act to intermeddle on either side. Hence Divines have been satisfied mostly to discover the general Duties in their Writings, and Preachers have undertaken little farther in their Sermons: each Sex being too ready to take offense, or scorn or ridicule anything that comes very close upon this subject. But, *illi robur & aes triplex circa pectus erat.*--- Our Author fearing neither One nor the Other, as if he had been made of Oak, and treble Brass about his heart, hath ventured his paper Pinnace amidst the Waves where two great Seas meet in such violent contentions as are stirred up in those miserable Families where they have shut the Fear of God out of doors.

Such unnatural heats make the life bitter; and, as an Ancient asserts, *Proxime ad ignis Infernalis cruciatus, acceder. dolores illos quos sentiunt quibus dispar conjugium contiget*: That is in plain English, *The evil effects of disparity in the Marriage state, is next to the torments in Hell fire*; which every person would be willing to prevent if he could, or at least to make the best of a bad Market. I would advise those that are under the temptation of Family-discords, if Scripture-precepts and examples are nothing with them, and the Divine authority of the Commands of the great God impress nothing upon them, (which would be very sad and dreadful in the account against them at the great Day) to consider but the brutish policy of a couple of Goats, that meeting in the midst of a narrow Bridge they were to pass over, had they contended which should give way, they had both fallen into the water; but one of them fairly lies down, and suffers the other to go over him, and so they were both preserved: And remember how excellent the Moral is of the two empty earthen Pots that were swimming upon the water with this Motto, *Si colledimur, frangimur; If we chance to clash, we ruin ourselves, and break one another all to pieces.*

But if the Families be pretending at least to the fear of God, and that have any sense or respect for their Redeemer that died for them, let them consider that Commission given to his Disciples at their mission into the wide world, Luke 10.5. *Into whatsoever house ye enter, first say, Peace be to this house; and if the Son of Peace be there, your peace shall be upon it; if not, it shall turn to you again.* We are to wish you peace, and pray for it; invite, exhort, command all Families to keep the peace: and if there be a Son of peace there, or a Son of the God of peace, our counsel will stick upon you; but if not, you are but where you were, unsubjected Children of Belial, and the peace we wished you will return to us again, to tender it to some other Family that will better regard the authority of our counsel. And upon this account this little Book is come abroad, and what entertainment it shall meet with in its travels, the event will soon discover.

It is too evident that the disorders in the more subordinate parts of the Family, as the undutifulness of Children and disobedience of Servants, are occasioned and fomented by the distempers in the head and vital parts. Hence this skillful and learned Family-Physician hath endeavored the cure and repair of the head and heart of those Families, not troubling himself so much with the small scratches found upon the inferior members. *Through the wisdom* (of the Head) *the house is built, and with understanding it is established*, Prov. 24.3. where this is wanting, that house is nigh to desolation, according to that of our Savior, Mat. 12.25. *A house divided against it self cannot stand.*

It were to be wished that Christians (especially under the ties of conjugal Relation) could learn to bear with one another's infirmities, and so fulfill the Law of Christ. A choleric Couple being asked, *how he and his Wife lived so comfortably and sweetly together?* The man answered, *When my Wife's fit is upon her, I yield to her; and the woman said, When my Husband's fit is upon him, I yield to him, and so we are never angry both at once.* It were well if the one were as David's Harp to appease the fury of the other: It seldom proves an unhappy Conjunction, when the one is deaf, and the other blind: the Man must not always hear, nor the Wife always see. *Love covers a multitude of sins*, Prov. 10.2. Neither can the Man's not doing his duty discharge the Wife from doing hers. A soft answer pacifieth wrath on both sides.

But the Author being large in these things, I only shall commend to you the practice of Domestic affairs. And first, there is a sinful quietness, a mere piece of Stoicism, when persons concern themselves with nothing, let things go how they will, having the use of no passions at all; for even the evenest weights are easily put into some unevenness, though they tend at last to a settlement in an even poise; and so the most even and sedate tempers are naturally prone to some little exorbitances, though they soon return to their quieted center. Paul, a very still man after his Conversion, and became *all things to all men, that he might gain some*, (though he was a rough piece before) *exhorting them all to meekness of Spirit*, Col. 3.12. That *they should put it on as a Garment*; implying, that they had as good a go without their Garments, as suffer themselves to be stripped of this Grace of Meekness: yet he could be in a flame, and stands up in the University of Athens, and in the open street reproves their Idolatry. So Moses the meekest man, yet he showed he could be moved upon a just cause, and at the sight of the Calf he fumes and flies out as if he had been a man made up of Salt and Gunpowder, rashly throws down the Tables of the Law, and breaks them all in pieces: And Christ himself, as meek as he was, could take a scourge of small cords, and whip the buyers and sellers out of his Father's house. Stillness in not Stoicism.

Secondly, There's a holy stillness or quietness of spirit, in all conditions, bearing that quietly which we cannot help possibly. This is my affliction, and I must bear it: It is a Grace of God's Spirit, Dove-like, like himself. Nature can't reach it, Philosophy can't teach it; Nature is a tetchy piece, full of choler. Saul, a turbulent Fellow, nobody that feared God could be at quiet for him: But when the Spirit of God came upon him, it made him as tame as a Lamb; and so 'twas prophesied, *When the Spirit should be poured forth, the Lion shall lie down with the Lamb*, Isa. 11.6. And it is made the Character of an understanding man, *He should be of an excellent Spirit, of a cool Spirit*: so the Hebrew, Prov. 7.27. A cool spirit in opposition to a hot spirit, is an excellent spirit, and an excellent spirit is a cool spirit. Indeed some new spirits are naturally cool without Grace, as many Heathens were, that had made a conquest over their natural tempers by improving their reasons, and fixing their resolutions; yet not being from the Holy Ghost, it can but pass for a natural Virtue in them, but never for a spiritual

Grace. This mystery is not learned at Athens, but at Jerusalem. None but God can give it, none but Christ can still the wind, and the waves of the turbulent Sea of unruly passions: therefore we must pray heartily, if we mean to live quietly.

Moreover, 'Tis not the quieting of the tongue only, if the mind be still unquiet. Some can pinch in their passion, when yet their minds are like the troubled Sea, and burn inwardly like fire put up, and this is more immediately the work of God. We say to a discontented person, Set your heart at rest, but 'tis God only can set the heart at rest: Nor would I have such fiery natures shelter themselves under Religious Privileges. What! a Religion that cannot bridle the passions, and bring the Soul to the foot of God! That is a poor Religion indeed! 'Tis a sad thing that God cannot lay a cross upon a man's shoulders, but the proud worm must show himself displeased, and the Almighty must look to himself: the Arrows of bitter words flying from him so thick and fast against the Providences of Heaven, God must know he will not bear it, he will not take it at his hands, he will not put it up.

Finally, I could wish this following Treatise might have entertainment in all sorts of Families; Quiet Families that enjoy the warm Sun and the serene Air in pure Love and Peace, how should they bless God for the ornaments of a meek and quiet spirit, while others are staked down in the Suburbs of Hell, restless Spirits, like the Inhabitants of tormenting Tophet! Unquiet Families, let them read and consider, and read it over and over again, if peradventure God may be merciful unto them, and still the unruly waves, having sent the means of it into their houses, and put it into their hands. If in anything it prove distasteful, and makes thee winch, attribute it not to the ill-preparedness of the Medicine, but the incurableness of the Distemper. If thou throw'st it away because it makes the wound smart, Fare well; Live in love and peace, and the God of love and peace shall be with you.

I should greatly rejoice if anything in the ensuing Treatise prove instrumental to establish Peace in Families, and be helpful to make up breaches between *Men* and their *Wives*. I know the Author's design is principally to promote this end, That would make this Discourse effectual to beget and maintain Love and Peace between *Men* and their *Wives*, is the hearty Prayer of,

R E A D E R,

Thy real Well-wisher,

J. R.

THE
Introduction

It is observed, That many Husbands and Wives that are eminent Professors of Religion, yea, such as are truly gracious as well as Professors, through the weakness of their Graces, and strength of their Corruptions, do live together in much discontent, and that there are often manifestations of Wrath and Discord between them; yea, and many times their passions grow to such an height, that in their anger they speak and do such things as do very much disparage their Professions, and discredit Religion, and cause the Enemies of Religion to speak evil of the ways of God, because of their disorderly carriages: Therefore I have endeavored in the ensuing Discourse to show the causes whence usually Wrath and Discord doth arise between them, and have shown which of them is most faulty when Wrath and discord happens. Also I have opened the evil of Wrath and Discord between such near Relations, and have laid down some Rules and Directions how they may prevent it for the time to come, and diverse motives to persuade them to use those Directions.

      Indeed it hath very much troubled me to observe the hot contests that have been between such relations, about very trifles; how some will be offended, and cannot tell wherefore: They have been of such choleric constitutions, that they have enquired after occasions to feed their anger: Alas! how much are such carriages unbecoming the Gospel! how much do such persons dishonor God, and prejudice their own Souls! The consideration thereof hath put me upon using my weak endeavors to gather such means out of the Word of God as may prevent their continuance in such disorderly carriages; that they may not any longer drink the Waters of *Meribah*, that is of Strife, (their common drink) lest they find them prove Waters of *Marah*, that is Waters of Bitterness, at last: I shall pray them to suspend their passions so long, as seriously to consider what I have written, that what they find agreeable to God's Word they would endeavor faithfully to observe.

AN ANTIDOTE AGAINST DISCORD BETWEEN *MAN* and *WIFE*

I. *Whence is it that Wrath and Discord between Husband and Wife doth arise?*

1.

Anger and Contention between Husband and Wife doth arise from a prevailing principle of flesh in the heart: a fleshly mind produceth much strife, and violent passionate disturbances, 1 Cor. 3.3. *For ye are yet carnal; for whereas there is among you envying, and strife, and divisions, are ye not carnal, and walk as men?* The meaning is, the flesh prevails in them more than the spirit; the remainders of old Adam are very strong in them: that party that is touchy, and takes distaste at every trifle, doth evidence, that much unmortified corruption remains in that heart; and I say, when distaste is taken at that which is not positive sin, then distaste is taken at a trifle. Now when corruption prevails in the heart, it will break forth, and blister upon the tongue, 'tis because a person is rotten in heart that he is rotten in language, as in Mat. 12.34. you may smell the filth of some men's hearts by their breath; and it is from this root, from this ground, that some persons are all for strife and debate: hereby strife is the very element wherein they live, and they live, and love to live, in troubled waters, yea also in the fire of trouble; they are persons of contentions. If their fleshly principle was not so prevalent, their passions would not be so violent: and it is sad when the strongest bent of some people are for strife, that they can discover the boisterousness of their spirits upon every frivolous occasion; and certain it is, that either Husband or Wife that is soonest angry with the other, is most carnal, for anger, wrath, variance, strife, contentions and hatred, are fruits of the flesh, and they are seldom separated, Gal. 5.20. So that a persisting in this disorder is a contrivance to fulfill the inordinate motions of inbred corruption. Now passion and contention is usually accompanied with carnal emulations, litigious strivings for trifling matters, enmity, variance, a muttering of disgraceful and opprobrious words: These usually go together, and raise a tempest of wrath, and by that violent commotion the person is transformed into a very beast; and these must needs be the fruits of the flesh, because they are directly opposite to the fruits of the spirit, which are love, peace, long-suffering, gentleness, goodness, meekness, etc. and those that bring forth the fruits of the spirit are able to moderate their anger, and can patiently bear, and forgive even many real injuries, and will not be provoked but for such just causes, and not more or longer than the word of God allows. So that it is evident that one ground of Wrath and Discord between such near Relations as

Husband and Wife, is the prevailing of a fleshly principle in the party that is more passionate.

    2. Self-love is a cause of Wrath and Discord between Husband and Wife, whereby the one party so inordinately loves itself, that it hath no true conjugal love for the other, that he or she never thinks of the injuries and indignities which he or she offers to the other, or else will suppose them to be none, or else lightly esteem of them as not worthy the recital, on the other side makes the party guilty of this self-love or defect of conjugal love, heinously to aggravate the injuries offered to itself, and so make huge Mountains of small Molehills, and causeth its heart easily to apprehend the wrong, and to be busy in meditating of it, being apprehended, and then longeth for revenge one way or other, wishing some disaster to fall upon person, or name, or both of the other, and are glad to be freed any way from the relation, thinking nothing sufficient to make amends for so great an indignity offered one of such worth as the party fondly and falsely conceits itself to be. And if the self-lover hath not so much respect given as is expected, is presently provoked to a furious rage. When a Wife is mastered by self-love, she over values her-self, and undervalues her Husband: she can wink at the injuries she offers her Husband, and put on spectacles of affection when she looketh on those wrongs which are offered to her, whereby it cometh to pass that every small matter seemeth a great injury, and provoketh her to great anger; whereas if she thought meanly of herself, and loved her Husband as herself, she would not have suffered herself to be over-balanced with the weight of self-affection in judging of the injury, nor in giving the reins to her anger to rise to such an height. If the Wife had an endeared love for her Husband, her love would have more force to restrain her from reproaching and reviling her Husband, than any injury or seeming contempt of her

could have to provoke her to anger. For love suffereth long, yea suffereth all things, and is not provoked to anger, 1 Cor. 13.4, 7. The prevailing of self-love, and the cooling and decay of conjugal love, is the fundamental cause of all disturbances that are between Husband and Wife; and that party that is most passionate, hath least conjugal affection; and by want of this love, small matters do exasperate, and breed distaste: and he or she that is most furious, is most faulty: For an Husband or Wife cannot have a bitter mind upon small provocations against one another, if they dearly love one another, and everything that provokes is a small provocation, which is not a breach of God's Law: And as they ought not to have a bitter mind, so where love is prevalent they cannot proceed to reviling words, or to averseness, or estrangedness, or any abuse of one another. And if a breach or wound be unhappily made, the balsamic quality of love will heal it: so that here you see that too much self-love, and too little conjugal love, is another cause of discord between Husband and Wife, and that party that is first provoked, and grows most furious, is most defective in Love.

3. Pride is another cause of Wrath and Discord between Husband and Wife: for it is the diseased temper of the heart that causeth dissentions, more than occasions or matters of offense do. A proud heart is troubled and provoked by every word or carriage that seems to tend to its undervaluing. A proud Woman is always jealous of her Honor and Reputation, is also very suspicious of contempt, so that the least seeming injury provokes her to choler and disdain, because she is ready to imagine that thereby she is exposed to contempt. Solomon saith, *Only by pride cometh contention*, Prov. 13.10. The meaning is, that Pride is good for nothing but to cause brawling, strife and contention. Pride alone of itself, without the aid of any other thing, is sufficient to kindle contention; yea, the wise man observed so much Strife and anger

to come from Pride, as that he seems to speak as if Pride was the only cause of all brawlings: so that the least spark of anger kindled with the smallest occasion, bursteth out into a raging flame of fire, if it be blown with the wind of pride or self-conceitedness. A proud humor that would have all stoop to it, if it meet with the least seeming slight, is presently hurried with unquiet and turbulent thoughts, which are fit Harbingers to prepare a lodging in the heart to entertain anger: And this is clear from the nature of Pride; for 'tis a fountain-sin, a root-sin, productive of many other sins; it nurseth, nourisheth, and bringeth up many other sins, and it is the mother of these three very bad Children: First, It makes men and women boast of Themselves, of their Wisdom, Parts, Accomplishments, and their Pedigree, as the proud Jews did when they were contending with Christ: Say they, We have Abraham to our Father: So some will say, *I am the Child of such a godly Father: I was such a man's Son or Daughter, or such a worthy man's Wife, and shall I be slighted now?* and so brings forth the second Daughter Contention, and be wrangling with any one that crosseth the proud humor, fret at anything that looks like an undervaluing, fume at, rage at, and revile any person that will not be observant of their wills, and cannot endure to be hindered from insulting and commanding: And this being the humor of many Husbands and Wives, it produceth and nourisheth their passions. But the third Daughter of Pride is Contempt. Proud persons do despise and vilify all whom they converse with: for some Wives despise their Husbands in their hearts, as Michal did David, that let Husbands carry it as obligingly as they can, yet because their Wives do despise their persons, they will despise their actions, and so be angry with everything that they do; they do despise their actions and company too with abhorrence, as the stomach doth meat which is offensive to it, and so like their Husbands like ill-savored meat. From this ground everything that their Husbands say or do is offensive to them: so fly at them with bitter and reproachful words; but the truly humble woman is not provoked to anger, though she be neglected, because her lowly conceit of herself makes her to think that she is not worthy to be much esteemed, nor yet is she angry, though she hath received an injury, because she thinks she hath deserved it, either by like faults committed against her Husband, or more heinous sins against God: so that it is clear that another great cause of that Wrath and Discord that is between Husband and Wife, is the pride of that party that is most passionate; And it is evident from the Scripture, that Pride is the chief ground of sinful anger, if we read Prov. 21.24. *Proud and haughty scorner is his name who dealeth in proud wrath.* So much inordinate passion as one hath, so much pride he or she hath; for pride is as much seen in frowardness and passion as in any thing, and there is a proportion between sinful passion and pride in everyone's heart; and that man or woman that hath a passionate spirit, hath a proud spirit, let them seem to be never so humble in other things; for the truly humble Soul is of a meek spirit, for Christ joins meekness and humility together, Mat. 11.29. *Learn of me, for I am meek and lowly.* I shall evidence to you in these following particulars how passionate and angry persons are proud persons, and how pride raiseth their angry passions.

First, Proud persons are impatient of being contradicted in their speeches, be they right or wrong: You must say as they do, and not gainsay them. So if passionate persons be opposed in what they say or do, they are in a flame presently. An angry person cannot bear the least contradiction.

Secondly, Pride makes persons uncharitable and censorious: They extenuate other persons Virtues and good Works, and suspect ungroundedly their sincerity: They will vilify others, and give them disgraceful terms. Thus will passionate persons do: They will judge the party that they are angry with, as a vile, base, unworthy person, and censure him for an Hypocrite, void of all inward and real good.

Thirdly, Pride causeth men and women to hate reproof. Those that are proud are forward in finding fault with others, but love not a plain reprover of themselves, as in Prov. 15.12. *A scorner loveth not one that reproveth him*. They can easily endure to be evil, and do evil, but not to hear of it. So passionate persons impatient of admonition, they will not endure to be told of their faults: They storm and rail at every reproof that is given them; their spirits are too hot to be told of their faults.

Fourthly, Proud self-conceited persons are ever talkative persons, and more desirous to speak than to hear: They will suffer none to speak but themselves, because such think always highly of their own understandings. So angry persons rage if any offer to discourse in their presence; if any presume to speak, they take exceptions at every word. If their passions are high, their first word of command is, *Hold your peace, and say no more, or be gone out of the Room*. They cannot endure the company of those that will adventure to reply to anything they say: They are too high to be answered again, though by their Equals and Superiors, and this kind of passionate rage is the effect of Pride.

Fifthly, If proud persons be wronged, they look for great submission before they will forgive: you must lie down at their feet, make very full confession, and behave yourselves with very great submission, or they will never pardon the offense you have done them: But if they have wronged others, they are hardly brought to confess that they have wronged them, and more hardly brought to be so humble as to desire a reconciliation. Thus it is with angry persons: while anger lasteth, no persuading them to pass by a wrong, but if ever they do forgive, it must be upon the humblest submission that may be, but never acknowledge any wrong that they do: Whatever abuse they do offer to another, is justified as well done. Such do think that they can do nothing amiss, and thus you see how pride, passion and frowardness do go together, that a contentious person is a proud person, and cannot put up injuries, and foul words. *He that is of a proud spirit stirreth up strife*, Prov. 28.25. What is people's wrath? what are their scorns, their railings, and endeavoring to vilify those that have offended them, but the foam and vomit of their Pride? It is so contentious a sin, that it makes Men and Women firebrands in the Societies where they live: There is no quiet living with them longer than they have their own saying, will, and way. They must bear the sway, and not be crossed; and when all is done, there is no pleasing them; for the missing of a word, or a look, or a compliment, will catch on their hearts, and raise their fury. As a little spark on Gunpowder will make it flame, so the least conceit of a disrespect offered, doth disturb their peace, break their sleep, and cast them into a Fever of passion. There are seldom any hot contests between Husband and Wife, but Pride doth occasion them. All the passionate, angry, irreverent, insulting, and insolent carriages of a Wife to an Husband, are from the pride of her heart, and hence it is that Pride makes Men and Women angry: Pride makes them think themselves superior in worth and goodness to any; so they think that they are too high to have their wills crossed by any; and say, *Shall I bear such a thing from thee, poor pitiful Creature?* And then proud persons think themselves so good, as they can never deserve any cross from another, and that whatever they do, deserves not contradiction at all; whereas they are ready to make misinterpretations of anything that another doth, but think that they can justify everything that they do: So that whatever is done by another that suits not with their proud humor, puts them into a fiery passion presently; for proud spirits make their wills to be the rule of their actions, and they would have it to be a rule of all other men's actions too: and such when their wills are opposed, cannot but be froward, and highly displeased. Also proud persons think nothing too mean for others to do, and so would fain put their Equals, yea their Superiors, to do such things as they scorn to touch; and if they be not complied with presently, they are in a flame of passion, and are froward and contentious presently: and thus you see how Pride doth bring forth anger, frowardness and contention.

4. Foolish niceness breedeth choler: for if you come into the house of one who is nice and curious, you shall easily perceive how soon she is incited to great anger upon a little cause. I instance in the Female Sex, because they are more influenced by niceness and curiosity than men, and therefore by it they are mostly provoked to fretting discontent. If the decking and adorning, ordering and cleansing of their house, be not fully answerable to their minds; if a spot or wrinkle be upon their Garments, they are enraged with anger, that the house will scarce hold them, or at least not contain their clamorous voices. Those curious folks are not only offended with injuries, but also with shadows and appearances. Such can carp at Gestures of the Body that they do not like, and fret at the words of their Husbands because they do not think them respectful enough to them. They judge their language rustic, and their carriages clownish, so are in no way genteel enough to please their humors, and upon this account fall into such a rage of passion, as if they had received some mortal wound. They are so prying and quick-sighted, that they will espy some things amiss, by which they will alarm the whole Family and break their Husband's and their own Peace: If a failing be

ever so little, they cannot overlook it, and be more enraged that some small Family-concern is neglected, than that their Family-worship is omitted, whereby *they can strain at Gnats, and swallow Camels*, Mat. 23.24. They can storm at small offenses committed against themselves, and take no notice of great wrongs done to God. Whereas others, who have not their minds effeminated with this nice curiosity, can easily pass over such trifling imperfections, and repel anger in far more violent assaults: So that a Wife's niceness in finding great fault with every frivolous matter, doth occasion much jarring and hot contests between her self and Husband, whereby a small spark of distaste doth kindle a flame of a violent passions.

 5. Lightness in believing what comes to the ear, and listening to tale-bearers, doth raise Discord and Strife between Husband and Wife. Prov. 26.20. *Without wood the fire is quenched, and without a tale-bearer strife ceaseth*. So that as wood is the fire's fit nourishment, so is a tale-bearer fit to beget and nourish anger between Husband and Wife; yea, a tale-bearer doth raise contention so high, as to make a Separation between Husband and Wife, as Solomon saith, *A whisperer separateth chief friends*. When an Husband or Wife gives a credulous ear to the lying suggestions of a pickthank tale-bearer, they will be incensed to such raging anger, that a great matter will not be sufficient to quench the heat thereof. There have been manifold experiences of great evils which have followed credulity, and listening after tale-bearers. David giving ear to the false report of Ziba, was moved to unjust anger against innocent Mephibosheth. There is no greater firebrand in the world than a tale-bearer. One Neighbour comes to a Wife, and saith, *Your Husband was at such a place, spent so much money there, spake such and such words there, did such and such actions there*. The Wife presently believes it, and is in a rage

presently. Some Servants will tell their Mistress, *My Master did thus and thus, and said so and so of you.* Credit is presently given to the information, and the flame of passion is presently kindled, though if the matter were rightly enquired into, the information would prove false. Some Wives will search and enquire after matter to feed their passions, and enquire of their Servants *What is your Master doing? what did he say of such a business?* and if they be informed that he said or did anything cross to their humors, or contrary to their approbations, their Spirits are hot presently, and you may see violence and fury in their eyes. If an Husband or Wife will give credit to every story that a tale-bearer brings them, they shall never live at peace with one another.

6. A peevish, froward, humorous constitution is another cause of Anger and Discord between Husband and Wife, and so they will be angry at bare surmises, when it is nothing but a surmise or fancy that they make and propound to themselves, and thereupon let out their anger, like the Dog that barketh at the shining of the Moon. Hence many are angry at their own fancy. A pettish froward heart will create causes of anger to itself, when there are none; nay, the power of their peevish and pettish humors is such, that they are angry for everything. Every trifle, every toy, anything in the world that falls out in the least manner against their minds, puts them into an anger. And indeed when Husband's or Wife's anger comes to be common upon every trifle, it makes their anger contemptible, and no one cares for it. Some think to gain more Authority in their Family by their anger, and make others more conformable to them by it; but in truth it makes themselves the more despised. You shall find your froward furious persons, that they will be angry with irrational insensible Creatures, and a pettish and froward Wife will be angry with one for the fault of another: If a Child displease her, she will be angry

with her Husband. Some persons have such froward and fretful natures, that they have Gunpowder-Spirits, that as soon as anything displeaseth them they fly in the faces of their nearest Relations: They are like dry wood that have all the Sap and Juice out of it, as soon as ever the fire comes to it is all on a flame: So Husband and Wives that have hasty natures, Sapless, and void of true Wisdom, as soon as ever they have any occasion, but a little fire, a little occasion, they are all on a fire presently. Persons that are of froward and peevish dispositions will manifest their anger before anybody, never considering whether it be a convenient season. The Husband will vent his anger against his Wife, and the Wife vent her anger against her Husband, though in the presence of Children or Servants, and through the violence of their passions they care not what time they vent their revilings and reproaches: And such furious persons will upbraid one another with their failings, whoever be present; they will not allow time to consider inconveniencies, they are of such hasty Spirits, and so will belch forth their passionate expressions in haste. Also persons of choleric Spirits they have no command of their Spirits to get them down when they are once up. Though the winds be still, the waves of the Sea are up and down a great while after: So it is with Husbands and Wives, when there is occasion to stir up their hearts to anger by reason of their froward peevish natures. Though they have that which satisfies them, yet they cannot be quiet for all that, but they are (like Salamanders) in the fire continually. There are many Husbands and Wives that have Dog-days all the year long. You know we have Dog-days in one time of the year, but they last but a little while; but indeed such Husbands and Wives that have humorsome natures and dogged dispositions, have always Dog-days: there is nothing but frowardness, wrangling and jangling between them all the year long; so that in many the heat of anger is in their hearts like the fire of Hell, that is unquenchable: If once their passion is up, they will never have done, as if the fire of Hell were in their hearts; and though there may be yielding to them, and a forbearing of all words that may feed their passions, yet nothing will quench them: And it is certain, that many that have suffered their passion and anger to arise unjustly and foolishly, and are convinced in their own consciences that there is no sufficient cause for their anger, yet they will continue in their anger, and abide in it, that they might not seem to others to be angry without a cause, and they are loath that the distemper of their hearts should be discovered. And also it appears that an Husband and Wife is swayed by a peevish, froward, choleric nature, when they can let their anger rise to its utmost height for a very little offense, that which would not be taken amiss at all by a person of meek Spirit. Also persons are swayed by a choleric nature, when they do manifest bitterness of Spirit in their anger: This bitterness of Spirit consists in this, when one is provoked, and passion is up against another, they care not what provoking speeches they use towards others, grating upon their Spirits such things as they know before, or at least hope will provoke them, and this they do very eagerly: Whereas one of a meek Spirit will be very loath to provoke anyone; and if there be any means to reform another without manifesting the passion of anger, he will do it. He will try all means of reformation before he will be angry. I say, though a meek person be justly offended by another, yet if he can reform him with sweetness of carriage he will do it: but the hearts of many Husbands and Wives are like a Sponge filled with Gall and Vinegar; if you do not touch it nothing will come out, but nip it between your fingers and it will presently come out in abundance: so many hearts, if you do but nip them as it were between your fingers, the Gall will presently drop down, they will presently be angry, as it is with many bodies, a choleric stomach will turn all meats, and make them to be bitter to them; and so it is with such Husbands and Wives that have choleric Spirits, the distemper of their hearts turn everything into bitterness, and if anything be done unto them that doth displease them, they'll go and chew upon it; and so embitter their own Spirits by thinking what wrong the other hath done him or her. A bitter Pill must not be chewed, but swallowed down whole: so when there is anything done amiss to Husband or Wife, the wrong indeed is a bitter Pill, and should be swallowed down. No marvel if every cross is so bitter if it be chewed and meditated on. Again, it is evident that an Husband or Wife is mastered by a choleric distemper, if either of them be of a fierce disposition, and indeed we may call such *harebrained Christians*, that are fierce and furious upon every occasion. An angry person is more furious when only a seeming injury is done to him or her, than when a real injury is done to God: so that many times some people's passions makes them like a furious mad Dog, that when it sets on an object it cannot be called back. Oh! the anger of froward peevish Spirits is very unruly: so that such angry persons have not only their passions grow to bitterness, fierceness and unruliness, but to Cruelty: they have passion without compassion; and many times the rage is so great, that the Wife (that is so much inferior to her Husband in strength) will not only give provoking speeches, but blows also. She will fly at his head, pluck him by the hair, strike him on the face, and throw anything that she hath in her hand at his head: Indeed here is an evidence of a choleric temper. But certainly all the anger of an Husband or Wife that doth not aim at the good of the party that he or she is angry with, is sinful anger, and is the effect of a furious disposition. And thus I have shown you as brief as I might the usual grounds that occasion wrath and discord between Husband and Wife.

II. *I come now to show the evil of Wrath and Discord between Husband and Wife, in these following particulars.*

1.

The gratifying an angry passionate humor produceth abundance of evil effects. All other passions do but draw men and women to evil, but anger doth precipitate them. If anything be the principle of evil, it is a froward Spirit which is the principle of anger: And therefore let us consider the effects of frowardness and passion, to see how much hurt it doth to the Souls of men and women.

1. When an Husband or Wife is angry, it doth mightily blind the judgment of that party that is so, and blind reason exceeding much. The heat of passion, the fire of passion, when it is kindled, causeth a great smoke to come up to the understanding and judgment, and even extinguish reason: Other Passions stray from Reason, but this treads it under feet, and leads it as it were in triumph. When once such near Relations as Husband and Wife are stirred, are froward, and in anger, they do things so irrationally, that one can hardly think them the same men and women that they are at other times, it doth so take away their reason. The man or woman that is froward cannot have any counsel, but run headlong, yea, run in a rage to such and such things, and know not what he or she saith or doth, because while passion is prevalent he or she hath no use of reason or understanding. *Passionate persons are rash and inconsiderate, they act without deliberation, they run headlong,* Job 5.14. That is, they go too fast forward; and they who will not take time to consult of what they are about to do, may have time to repent of what they have done, and all this

happeneth because the passion of anger causeth a cessation of the exercise of reason. Other things may dazzle the sight of reason, but this makes it stark blind, and for a time maketh men and women as it were distracted, and out of their wits. Anger having obtained the sovereignty over their minds, taketh away all judgment, counsel, and reason, and over-swayeth all by foolish affection and raging passion, and by darkening reason. It is a kind of short madness, saving that here it is far worse, in that the person that is possessed with madness is necessarily (willy-nilly) forced to be subject to that fury; but a sinful angry passion is entered into wittingly and willingly. Madness is the evil of Punishment, but Anger is the evil of Sin. Madness as it were thrusteth Reason from its Imperial Throne, but Anger abuseth Reason, by forcing it with all violence to be a slave to Passion, so fit to execute those works of darkness in which Rage employeth it. *Well then, O Husband! or thou, O Wife! seeing thy immoderate anger is an injury to humanity, and a Rebel against the Government of Reason, that it is without Reason, and against Reason; Remember then that thou art a Man, or Woman, and do thou scorn to subject thy self to such bestial fury. O with how much attentive care should'st thou avoid anger: and notwithstanding provocations offered thee, do not disturb the quiet of thine own mind. Therefore give not way to anger, seeing it blindeth reason, which is the light and guide of the Soul. If men abhor Drunkenness, and that worthily, because it maketh them differ from brute Beasts only in shape of body: why should'st thou not for the same cause hate this Vice of Anger, which like a burning Ague doth so disturb thy mind, and while the fit lasteth it uttereth nothing but raving? Do not then nourish thy froward humor, nor give way to thy wrath. Be not of an hasty Spirit, whereby thou art guilty of such rashness and fierceness in all thy actions, because those furious actings are so contrary to right Reason.*

2. Another effect of Anger and Discord between Husband and Wife is, that they are great enemies to the quiet of their own hearts. An angry passion is a great disturber of a man or woman's own peace. That we may say of it as the wise man saith of Cruelty. Prov. 11.17. *He that is cruel troubleth his own flesh.* So those that are of froward Spirits, they trouble their own flesh, and trouble their Spirits too: It doth macerate and vex the Soul with fury; for what greater torment can we imagine, than to have the mind distracted upon the Rack of Rage? As therefore we would account him a mad man, who with his own hands should set his house on fire, and consume it, alike mad is that person to be thought, who will set his or her Soul on fire with the raging flame of anger, wherein it is not only tormented in this life, but also (without Repentance) in the life to come it shall be tormented everlastingly. Rage and fury tortureth more than wrong or injury! Hereby men and women prove burdens to themselves, and hence it is that an angry Husband or Wife cries out, *No one is so plagued as I am, I know no body so crossed as I am*, because indeed they are plagues to themselves and crosses to themselves, they having no quiet in their own Spirits, nothing without is quiet to them. If we could look into the bosom of an angry person we should find that there is no such discontented Spirit as an angry Spirit is; such an one would fain have his or her own will; but sailing herein, in spite of his or her heart there will be nothing but confusion and trouble in his or her Spirit. Immoderate anger hath proved an enemy to the body itself: it inflammeth the blood, stirreth up diseases, and breedeth such a bitter displeasedness in the mind as tends to consume the strength of Nature, and hath cast many into acute, and many into chronic sicknesses, which have proved their death. And how uncomfortable kind of death is this? Well then, let the party that is most overcome by this passion say, *What good do I*

get by this passion? What! had it not been better for me to have put up this wrong, than endure such vexation to myself, and be guilty of doing my body so much prejudice as to cause me (if I continue my anger) to fall into the Diseases of Melancholy, Frenzy, Madness, Apoplexy, Palsy, and Falling-sickness, which are the usual effects of this prevailing Distemper of furious passion? O then shall I be angry upon every trifling occasion, and offer my body and spirit such great injuries? No, I will not; for I cannot pretend to hope for any inward or outward comfort by my anger; nay, my passion doth not only impair the health of my body, but mightily deform my body: it deforms my countenance, and takes away the amiable sweetness of it, which appeareth in a calm and loving temper. I should loathe myself, should I view my Picture while I was in my fury, before the frowning wrinkles and inflamed blood had returned to their place, and had left my visage to its natural comeliness. Is it not then better to forget injuries, pass by wrongs, bear with some opposition, and deny the gratifying of my will, than do my Body and Spirit so much prejudice, and lose that contentment and sweetness, that by meekness I might enjoy, and lose that inward peace and satisfaction of mind that otherwise I might have, or deprive myself of that beauty and comeliness, that otherwise I might preserve? O then, God forbid that I should gratify my angry humor.

3. An angry person is very troublesome to others, even to the whole Family wherein that angry person dwells, and all those that do converse with him or her, When the Husband or Wife is angry or froward, O how extremely burdensome is he or she to that Family; that Solomon saith in two places, Prov. 21.9, 19. *that it is better to dwell on the house-top, or in the Wilderness, than to dwell with a brawling woman in a wide house.* She is such a vexation to all those with whom she dwells. He instanceth in a woman, because that Sex is most subject to this brawling kind of life: They

are most apt to be angry and contentious. An angry Husband or an angry Wife is a torment to all those that live in Family; and therefore the Holy Ghost by Solomon saith, in Prov. 22.24. *Make no friendship with an angry man, and with a furious man thou shalt not go.* There is no good to be gotten by the company of one that is usually angry upon every trifling occasion: There is no peace to be enjoyed in angry person's company. A froward Spirit troubles his own house; and consider what is said of such an one in Prov. 11.29. *He that troubleth his own house, shall inherit the wind*: that is, as he or she hath been a trouble to his or her own house, so God should blast that person in all his or her ways. Indeed passion is so troublesome between Man and Wife, as they can hardly dwell together under one Roof, because they spend a great part of their life in troubling one another. By their passions they are vexatious to one another, and in their house it is stormy weather all the year long, that it is a very rare thing to enjoy any calm weather in the Family where angry persons dwell. Hence it is that Husband and Wife can seldom eat their meat together at one Table without quarrelling, because their lives are so uncomfortable one to another, their company is very uncomfortable to others. Passion is an unruly thing, and therefore troublesome wherever it comes. And wilt thou then, O Husband or Wife! cherish that evil humor in thee, that will make thee a burden to all that converse with thee? If thou continuest to be angry upon every slight opposition or contradiction, thou wilt be had in contempt of all that are near thee: they will despise thy person, because thou dost break their peace, and deprive them of their quiet. So then if thou hast any desire to preserve the peace and quiet of thy house, and have any esteem of those that live with thee, do thy utmost endeavor (by the assistance of the Spirit) to mortify thy angry passions.

4. The prevailing of anger and contention between Husband and Wife doth destroy their love: there is thereby a great decay of the affection of love, and an augmentation of the passion of hatred. Anger makes persons guilty of slighting, despising, disrespecting and undervaluing those they should highly value, love and esteem; and this appears in the following particulars:

1. When persons are enraged that God's Providences do thwart their humors, they are offended and displeased with God, and their love to God doth very much abate; for where love to God is ardent and prevailing, there every Providential act of God is kindly accepted, and taken in good part. Such persons as love God, are well pleased with every dispensation of God, and are contented with every condition God puts them in: but when they are offended that God doth not give them everything according to their own will, when they do not like of God's disposing of them in this relation, or in this condition of life, and in this place of habitation; and begin to vex and fret themselves, be angry, and in a furious passion, that God doth not order things to their liking. Then their murmurings and repinings their vexing and fretting, their disgust and discontent, their anger and displeasedness of mind, doth exceedingly abate their affections to God. They begin to disrespect God more and more; they entertain conceits as if God did do them wrong in not ordering all things according to their humor; in their anger murmur that God yoked them to such Consorts, wishing that God had otherwise disposed of them. And knowing that all conjugal Relations are of God's ordering and appointment, they complain highly as if he had dealt injuriously with them in appointing such a Relation for them; and hereupon their love to God declines, and they care not for God's company, slight those duties and services wherein they might converse with God, and are more displeased with the seeming offenses they

pretend are done them by their Husbands and Wives, than for the neglect of God's worship, and indeed love grows cold to one whose company is not delighted in, for all persons take delight to be much in company of their beloved, and when God's company is not prized, he is not loved.

Now, seeing anger and discord doth lessen people's love to God, it must needs be the greatest evil, as it doth cause a decay of love to the chiefest good. The want of love to God is the most comprehensive and odious sin, it is the life of all particular sins. To be defective in love to the God of love, the fountain of love, the felicity of the Soul, is a sin not to be pardoned to any till it be repented of, and partly cured. *Therefore stay, O man, or O Woman! to what an height doth thy angry passion make thee to ascend? Dost thou not tremble to think how much thou dost provoke God, when thou dost in thine anger slight and disrespect God, and art angry with God because thou art displeased with thy Husband or with thy Wife, and because God's Providences do not suit thy humor? If his anger be dreadful when kindled but a little, what is it then when kindled very much? Here is the sad effect of thy being angry with thy Husband or Wife: thou then ventest thy froward humor upon God, and beginnest to quarrel with God for ordering such a Relation for thee, and beginnest to abate thy respects to God, and carest not to exercise thy self in those exercises wherein thou mayest enjoy God's company. Do not then feed thy angry passions, whereby thy heart is so much estranged from God, and whereby you thrust God from your hearts. Oh how should'st thou loathe thy violent passions and contentions, when thou considerest how they deaden thy affections to God! May not God justly thrust thee from his presence, when by thy wrath and fury thou dost thrust him from thy heart? If thou would'st preserve in thee a principle of prevailing love to God, endeavor after meekness and quietness of Spirit. As Husband and*

Wife are the nearest Relations, let them not be jarring and quarrelling one with another.

2. The prevailing of furious angry passion in a person doth abate true and real love to itself, By the rashness and inconsiderateness of people's wrath, they manifest no pity to themselves: Through the violence of anger how many have been cruel to themselves! they wound themselves, and must not that be dreadful that makes persons offer violence to themselves? Persons in their anger are not sensible how much mischief they do themselves: They will not allow themselves time to deliberate or consider of the prejudice that comes to themselves, by giving way to their anger, by neglecting to endeavor to suppress it. O what cruelty is this for persons to vex and torture themselves! O then what an heinous evil is it for people to let anger to rest in their bosoms. *Bethink thy self, O Man, or O Woman, of the danger of letting thy Spirit to be enraged with passion against thy nearest Relation for every trifle; Thou thinkest only to manifest the height of thy displeasure against thy Husband or against thy Wife, but indeed thou dost hurt thy self, and dost evidence that thou hast so little love to thy self, as thou hast no tender regard of thine own good. If thou didst really love thy self, thou wouldst carefully avoid whatever did prejudice thy self; thou wouldst faithfully watch against every thing that would break thy peace, or deprive thee of thy amiableness, or deform thee with a tart, sour, and furious countenance. And as hereby thou dost make it appear that thou dost not love thy self, by undervaluing a calm and quiet spirit, so thereby nobody will love thee. Thy passions do cause others to cease manifesting respects to thee; they make others to slight thee, and shun thee. If thou canst not live in quiet with thy Husband or Wife, nobody will esteem thee: so then passion and contention between Husband and Wife must needs be a very great evil.*

3. Anger will abate thy love to the person that thou art angry with. The decay of thy love to the party with whom thou art angry, doth appear in misinterpreting his actions in the worst sense, raising contention from suspicion or imagination, inventing causes of displeasure where none are. Thus by anger charity is notably violated, for love suffereth all things, therefore their love is small that will suffer nothing. Love covereth a multitude of sins, they therefore that find faults where they are not, rather than cover them where they are, do plainly show their want of love to the party with whom they are angry. It is the nature of love to make *great* faults seem *little*, and *little* faults *none at all*: but when a person's anger makes every slip in his or her Friend or Relation a capital offense, then there appears a great decay of love. When a person apprehending itself highly wronged by another, doth presently begin to slight that party, that person doth manifest more displeasure against the person he or she is angry with, than the offense, and hath no love at all for him. Such is the violence of passion, that there is scarce any other affection so strong, which it doth not easily subdue. Love is said to be stronger than Death; yet anger, if it be once admitted to rage, easily overcometh it: Persons then forget the love of the Relation that they are in. In anger Wives speak to their Husbands as if they had no kind of superiority at all, or as if God had not set them over them any way; so own neither subjection nor reverence to be due unto them, and so causeth them, instead of the duties of love, to bring forth the fruits of hatred. When the furious flame of anger is kindled in the hearts of some people, they care not what reproach they cast upon, or any other prejudice that they do unto those that they should love as themselves. Indeed this is the evil effect of anger, that it inclineth persons to hurt them that make them angry, that it putteth hurting thoughts into their minds, and

hurting words into their mouth, and inclineth them to think, or do some mischief. *And wilt thou favor that passion that tends to extinguish thy love to thy nearest and dearest Relation, that makes thee neglect to manifest those respects that belong to thy Husband or to thy Wife? If thou art a Wife, anger will put thee upon usurping authority over thy Husband, denying subjection to him that the word of God requires; make thee insolent and irreverent, and herein it makes thee oppose the word of God, which commands thee in all things to acknowledge thy Husband's superiority, by being obedient to him in all things in the Lord, that is in all things that are not positively sinful. If thou wert humble and meek, thou wouldst not be of such a captious, contentious and wrangling disposition, but overlook those failings that provoke proud spirits.*

Thus it is evident how anger hath a tendency to extinguish the love of God, for the love of God will not kindle and flame in an unquiet breast. It makes men and women fret against God, and murmur at his Providences, and makes them discontented with that state, and Relation he hath put them into, and that it abates people's love to themselves, and makes them desperate in their ways, makes them ready to mischief themselves, that is, makes them run upon such ways and courses as are likely to prove mischievous to them, without all love or pity to themselves. Be not then such an enemy to thy self, as to nourish such fiery passions in thee, as will do thy self the greatest prejudice. Also anger abates people's love to their nearest Relations, makes them entertain jealousies and suspicions which feed their anger, makes them take in ill part every light action, and so their hearts grow estranged from their dearest friends, and have their nearest Relation in contempt. *Thou then that dost find thy self by nature prone to anger, labor earnestly with thy self that thou mayest contain thine anger for a longer time. Enter into a resolve in the strength of divine assistance, that whatever occasions may be offered thee, yet thou wilt refrain to manifest thy wrath and displeasure, and so by little and little thou shalt attain an habit of patience and meekness.*

    5. In those that are guilty of much furious passion, their anger doth cause abundance of sin, as in Prov. 29.22. *An angry man stirreth up strife, and a furious man aboundeth in transgression.* Anger is the door and gate of Vice, and therefore the Psalmist saith, Psal. 37.8. *Cease from anger, leave off wrath, fret not thy self to do evil*; as if he would imply that to abound in anger is to abound in sin, and it cannot be but a person must be guilty of much sin, that lives in fretting passion and inward unrest. More sin is committed by a person in a fit of passion in one quarter of an hour, than a meek-spirited man commits in a quarter of a year. Moses in his zeal for God broke the two Tables of Stone whereon the Law was written, and sometimes passionate and angry people in their wicked heats of spirit break all the ten Commandments, and in most fits of passion they break in pieces most of the Commandments of the second Table. People's vile, wicked and sinful lusts, when they are pleased, stir not. But when once the heat of anger doth arise, that warms these lusts; they then (like Snakes warmed with the Sun) hiss and spit upon those that are about them. When there is a Land-flood that the Brooks get over the banks, and overflow the Meadows, they carry with them a great deal of soil, and a great deal of filth.

    Thus it is in an overflowing of all affections, but especially in the overflowings of the affection of anger there comes a great deal of filth along with it; for when once by rage the eye of reason is blinded, the angry person is easily led into a gulf of all wickedness. *He that is of an hasty spirit exalteth Folly*, Prov. 14.29. that is, exalteth wickedness. When persons are quick, and short of spirit, they are transported into many indecencies, which dishonor God, and wound their consciences. If men and women do not check their precipitant motions, by delay and due recourse to reason, they will be guilty of abundance of wickedness. For motions vehement, and of sudden eruption, run away without a rule, and end in folly and inconvenience. Prov. 14.17. *He that is soon angry dealeth foolishly.* By frequent fits of passion anger is concocted into malice, which doth evidence a very wicked disposition, and is found only in the most depraved natures. James saith, cap. 1.20. *The wrath of man worketh not the righteousness of God;* Intimating that it is so far from working righteousness, that it worketh all manner of evil. There is in a person's anger somewhat of rage and violence, which vehemently exciteth the person to act, and taketh away the rule according to which he or she ought to act: So anger causeth people's conscience to be stained with the impurities of their lives.

1. Violent passions cause Men and Women even to fly in the very face of God, and walk frowardly towards him, which God complains of in Isa. 57.17. *And went on frowardly in the way of his own heart.* When every Providence doth not suit with persons humors, or if their Husbands or Wives do cross them, they will be in a pettish humor against God, fall out with God for permitting such things to befall them; and so out of a pettish humor they lay aside, and have no mind to set upon any duty that they owe to God. And when God's dealings are at any time opposite to thy will, and permits any to molest thee, thou complainest that God hath dealt hardly with thee. Certainly there must needs be a very malignant humor in thee that makes thee act thus frowardly against God; and how sad is it for men and women by the violence of their passions against their nearest Relations, to act frowardly against God? *O thou Husband or Wife! thou art angry with thy Husband or with thy Wife, and wilt thou manifest thy frowardness*

against God? and because thy Husband provokes thee, wilt thou provoke God? because he injures or wrongs thee, wilt thou injure and wrong God? What infinite unreasonableness is this? What boldness and presumption is this? There is so much evil in it as is impossible for any to utter, it is so abominable.

2. When men or women are in fits of anger one with another, when the Wife falleth out with the Husband, the fear of the great and dreadful Majesty of God, the infinite God, and the dreadfulness of the fear of God is all gone, and she is bold upon sin, she cares not what she saith or what she doth, she fears not God's displeasures while the fit of passion and contention lasteth, for the fear of God is to depart from evil, and there can be no restraint from sin when that is gone. In people's fits of angry passions their reproachful and reviling speeches do much dishonor God, and their actions flatly oppose his will. While they are angry they do not stand in awe of God, and thereby their unruly Lusts are let loose, running up and down doing mischief, sinning against God and their Brethren. Indeed the gratifying of passionate humors doth make persons cease fearing God; in fearlessness of God is a mighty provoking sin. See what Almighty God saith in Jer. 5.22. *Fear ye not me, saith the Lord? will ye not tremble at my presence?* And in verse 24. *Neither say they in their hearts, Let us now fear the Lord our God.* And in verse 29. *Shall I not visit for these things, saith the Lord? shall not my soul be avenged on such a Nation as this?* O then be sensible what great provoking sins anger and contention do occasion?

6. Husbands and Wives by the frequency of their angry passionate fits make themselves all their lives contemptible to others. Some Husbands and Wives think to be terrible to others in their passion, but they discover so much folly, as that they make those that they are angry with to despise them: They may

think to gain the more authority, and make others stand more in awe of them, by their being angry with them; but they see so much rashness and distemper in their passion, that nothing deprives them of their authority and respect more than this constant passion of anger, when small matters puts them into a fiery fit. Indeed if persons did but observe their shameful carriages when they are in passion after they were come to their right minds, and in a calm frame of spirit did but consider how much they were disdained and contemned for it, it would make them ashamed of their anger. However, many are angry because they would not be despised, but keep others in subjection to them; yet nothing in truth doth work base esteem and disregard in the minds of those that they are angry and displeased with, than immoderate and common anger. Frequency of Husbands' and Wives' passionate fits mightily blazeth abroad, and discovereth their shame and folly, which occasioneth their contempt, as Wisdom causeth Honor and Respect. When Husbands' and Wives' anger, and (the effects thereof) clamorous brawling, and sometimes fighting, are usual and common, as well for trifles as weighty matters, persons do desperately contemn both, when they have no hope to prevent either. *If thou, O Husband, or O Wife, would'st have the better'dness of thy displeasure, have any effectual operation upon the mind of the party with whom thou art displeased for the purging away faults and vices, thou must manifest thy displeasure as the Physicians administer strong Physic, only upon extraordinary cases; for if Physic be commonly taken, it will have no extraordinary effect. If thou dost habituate thy self to the use of Physic in a common way, as thou dost thy food, it will not benefit thee in times of sickness; so if thy anger be frequent and common, it will neither do good to thy self or another; it will not be regarded.* The frequent brawlings of an angry person do but make him the scorn of others. That person that will not let pass any rumor or report that is spread of him or her, without reasonings and stir, doth expose him or her self to the more reproach: for they that cannot rule their own spirits, deserve no respect, because (as Solomon saith, Prov. 25.28.) *He that hath no rule over his own spirit, is like a City broken down, and without walls*; who is able to defend himself against no assaults, therefore every one slights him.

7. If an Husband or Wife doth manifest much passion, frowardness, and discontent against the other, the prevailing of such corrupt humors will hinder the angry, froward, and discontented, contentious, wrangling person from doing any good. A person in a froward temper is exceedingly indisposed to any good work. When thou wilt seem to aim at the glory of God, and yet wilt show thy self very passionate, know God hath no need of thy wrath: It is true he hath need of thy Zeal, but that is not thy wrath and passion, to break out in outrageous speeches, or railing bitter language; God hath no need of this wrath of man. Let persons have never such excellent parts, yet they will not be able to do any good almost, if they be froward; but they are like unto a Candle wet with salt Brine, they spit up and down, and are very unuseful in the places where they live.

1. The prevailing of anger in any persons, the indulging and gratifying an humorous spirit, indisposeth them to do good to themselves. Angry persons will be averse to commune with their own hearts, and to consider their own ways, or to search out their own disorders of life. The Wife is so transported with disgust against her Husband, that she apprehends to have displeased her, that she can think of nothing, or talk of nothing, but what may vilify or reproach her Husband; she will not do so much good to herself as to try whether those carriages correspond with the Divine rule, whether she can justify what she saith or doth to her

Husband by a warrant from God's word. She will not consider whether she hath not been transported into indiscreet and indecent excesses, or whether she would not have condemned such violent heats in another as she hath manifested. What I speak of one Sex here, I intend of both; so I proceed. People's frowardness and passion hinders them from doing good to themselves, as to farther the convincing themselves of the evil that they have done, and bringing them to repentance for it. *And wilt thou then dare indulge thy angry passions, that make thee incapable of doing thy self good? Most men aim at self-interest, self-advantage, and self-applause; but thou by thy passions dost disable thy self from doing any act advantageous to thy self, either to promote thy spiritual good, present profit, or present credit. Surely that temper of spirit must needs be very evil, that hinders thee from doing good to thy self.*

2. Thy frowardness and angry passion, thy contentious wrangling spirit hinders from doing any spiritual good; it indisposeth thee for performance of any spiritual duty to God; it makes thee averse to converse with God, and unfit to serve God in a right manner; it is an hindrance of holy Prayer. Angry persons cannot call upon God in a serious spiritual manner, because their hearts are carnal, earthy, and poisoned with self-love; nor will God hear them if they call upon him. Anger hinders persons in all ordinances, it makes them the most unfit persons in the world for to pray: therefore the Apostle saith in the 1 Tim. 2.8. *I will therefore that men pray every where. How? lifting up holy hands, but without wrath.* O Husband! or O Wife! thou must be sure when thou liftest up thine hands to prayer, that there be no wrath in thy spirit, that thou do not go to prayer in a passion. Angry passionate Prayers are vain Prayers. The Lord loveth zeal, and much warmth of affection in prayer, but he cannot abide wrath or the least spark of passion in prayer; a peaceable heart is as necessary in prayer,

as a pure hand. When a Wife coming to God in prayer, hath I know not what wrathful disputes within herself against her Husband, how can she look for a gracious acceptance with God? the like may be said of the Husband. Will the Lord be pleased with those that nourish secret displeasure against their nearest Relation? No, no, furious and unquiet thoughts must be laid down by those that would have favor with God, and compassions from God. If persons would compass God's Altar, and there offer up the Sacrifice of Prayer and Thanksgiving, they must first *wash their hands in innocency*, Ps. 26.6. And our Savior Christ commandeth, that *before persons offer any gift unto the Lord, that they seek to be reconciled to the party with whom they are displeased*, Mat. 5.23. So long therefore as any continue in their anger, they are unfit to pray; and this appears most manifestly in the fifth Petition of the Lord's Prayer, where we desire *to be forgiven as we forgive*, Mat. 6.12. And again, our Savior Christ doth single this out of all the other Petitions; but if you will not forgive men their trespasses, no more will your Father forgive your trespasses. They who are suing for and expecting favor and mercy from God, have need to discharge themselves of all wrath and displeasure towards men. And the Apostle Peter in the 1 Peter. 3.7: exhorts Man and Wife *to live together in love, that their prayers be not interrupted.* Jarrings between such Relations do hinder their praying together to any good purpose; therefore if you would be fit to go to God together for mercy and favor, beware that you carry no wrath in your hearts towards one another, for then you will be sent empty away: And is not that a very great evil, and too bad to be harbored in the hearts of Husbands and Wives, that will hinder them from enjoying fellowship and acceptance with God in prayer, that will either make them cease to pray together, or if they do pray will make their Prayers vain and fruitless, as passion and discord usually doth? Also anger and discord is a very great evil in hindering Husbands and Wives to do good, by unfitting them to come together to the Sacrament of the Lords Supper. I question not but many angry Husbands and Wives are convinced in their own consciences that they ought not to come to the Sacrament in a passion, when they are angry with one another; they know they must lay aside wrath and malice then, and be in charity with all persons. Hence many Husbands and Wives will rather lose a Sacrament, than come in a passion. Many will say, *I could not come to the Sacrament because my Husband and I fell out, or my Wife and I fell out*: Now this is a vile thing, that when there is a Sacrament that Men and their Wives are convinced that they ought to come unto, but the breaches that are between them hinder them. So many men and women by giving way unto their passions are unfit to hear and read the word, unfit for any act of obedience of the Divine Will, unfit for any act that hath a tendency to promote the Glory of God. So that the violence of passion doth hinder Men and Women from doing of any spiritual good.

 3. Passion and frowardness doth hinder Husbands and Wives from doing good to one another, it disables them from admonishing one another of any fault, because an admonition is to be administered in a spirit of meekness. A furious person is very unlikely to convince another of sin, neither hath such an one any heart to give another whom he or she is disgusted with, any spiritual counsel. That secret prejudice which is harbored in the angry person's breast, hindereth him or her from doing any offices of love for his or her nearest Relation; but instead of doing such a Relation good, will do him or her the greatest prejudice that may be done. Angry persons are no way servicable to the good of others, rather offering indignities than kindnesses to them. Here is a sore evil indeed, that angry Husbands and angry Wives are

neither serviceable to God, themselves, nor one another. *O then do not let thy passion rage for every trifle: thou then makest thy self unfit either for the service of God or man; and what a sad thing is it to be a useless Creature, not capable of doing any good! Oh then it is a sad and sore evil to be an angry, passionate, froward, and contentious person.*

8. Anger, passion and frowardness of spirit hinders persons from receiving any good. A froward spirit is unfit to take in any good; there is no dealing with angry and froward Spirits when they are in their fits, as there is no Physic to be given to a man when he is in the heat of his Fever, so there is no meddling with angry persons when they are in a flame: You must come to them when they are quiet, or else you will not be able to do them any good; and indeed this is the horrible distemper of this passion, that God and man must stay till it be down, that God should not only wait on persons to do them good, but also wait upon their wicked, vile, base Lusts, that he must stay till they are over before they are fit to hear him speak to them. Now it is a meaner thing to wait upon a person's humor, than to wait upon the meanest Creature in the world. When the fire of anger is kindled in people's hearts, they are fit to hearken to nothing; their souls are on fire, and not fit to hear anything: thus men's angry passions hinder them from receiving good. And an angry person is impatient of admonition, which is ordained of God as a means of their recovery from sin. Angry persons will fly in the face of a reprover; they cannot endure to have their ways and actions found fault withal; the more you endeavor to convince them of their sin, the more they are exasperated; the more you persuade them from their evil course, they grow the more furious in their passion, they are not fit to receive any good counsel; while they are angry they are obstinate and resolute; if you smite with a Reproof, 'tis as if you had

struck upon an Anvil, it makes no impression on them. And also anger is the cause that the word of God becometh unprofitable. Anger causeth men to entertain the truths of the word of Life, as wind in the stomach doth wholesome meat, that will not suffer it to enter. Those that will benefit by hearing God's word, *must be slow to wrath*, James 1.19. For anger hardens the heart, that the Seed of Life cannot take root, or leave impression, yea it makes resistance to the Work of Grace. Those Spirits in whom there is a wrathful fierceness, rise up in rage against the Word of God. Angry Spirits think that the Minister raileth, when he doth but discover their guilt to them; so people's passions stir them up many times to a fierce opposition of the Truth; but let such consider, that their perverse opposition with be their ruin, as in Luke 7.30. *they rejected the counsel of God against themselves*, that is, to their own loss. Though anger may not altogether hinder or keep them back from hearing, yet it will fully hinder them from practice; for then only persons receive good by the Word, when they practice what they hear, when they are *doers of the word, and not hearers only. O Husband! or O Wife, dost thou observe what an hindrance thy froward and passionate spirit is to thy receiving good? Indeed it is a sore evil to indulge thy self in that humor, which resisteth those means that should do thee good, whereby thou receivest no benefit by any means that is used for thy good; yea, the allowing thy self in thy passions doth deprive thee of the good thou hadst before; thou art not only hindered from receiving more good, but thou shalt lose even what thou hast.*

  It is reported that some Pearls may be dissolved by Vinegar; so there are many excellent things in men and women, but they are dissolved by the Vinegar of passion: the Vinegar of passion doth stain the spirits of men and women, and causeth them to lose that Beauty that they had before, yea, to lose much of the sweetness of the enjoyments of God himself, yea, it makes them lose the sense of Divine Love. As we cannot discern the Sun when we are near a scorching fire, so the Heavenly heat of Divine Love is not felt, if the furious flame of anger be kindled in people's hearts. Froward Christians have little sense of God's love towards them. *O then, O Husband! or O Wife! Do thy continual brawling hinder thee from receiving good by admonitions, counsels, and all ordinances, and make the means of Grace ineffectual to thee? Do they deprive thee of the good thou hast, and deprive thee of the light of God's countenance? Do they cause the withdrawing of the light of God's countenance? O then, what an evil thing is it for thee to be angry with thy Husband or thy Wife upon every trifle!* Thus I have opened the great evil of contentions between Husband and Wife, in showing the evil effect of their anger and discord between each other.

2. *Consider, O Husband! or O Wife! Anger is a sore evil, because thy angry fits of passion do grieve the spirit of God. Though by venting the froth of thy froward passionate spirit thou may'st please thy self, yet thou grievest the Holy Spirit. It is an ill thing to grieve thy friend; and indeed none are more grievous to their dearest Friends and nearest Relations, than froward and passionate people. When thy Friend comes to thy Family, and sees thee in a froward and passionate temper, it grieves him, and thou grievest the heart of thy Husband: It may be also he goes and complains of it to God, and thou grievest thy Friend, and he complains of it: but this is worst of all, thou grievest the spirit of God. When thou art in a fit of passion, the Spirit of God goes away to Heaven sadly, as it is in Ephes. 4.30, 31.* And grieve not the holy Spirit of God. Let all bitterness, and wrath, and anger, and clamour, and evil speaking, be put away from you, with all malice. *The Apostle unto that command, grieve not the Spirit, immediately subjoineth this, let all*

bitterness, etc. be put away; intimating that otherwise they could not cease from grieving the Holy Spirit.

Here are mentioned various degrees of anger, and every one of them doth grieve the Spirit. By *bitterness of Spirit* is understood the lowest degree of sinful anger, and also by *Bitterness* is understood all secret smothered displeasure, and alienation of affection, which hath more of discontent and grudge than of revenge. The next degree is wrath, or fierceness of Spirit, which is an impetuous rage, and passionate commotion of the heart and affections, upon the sense of an apprehended injury, preventing and obstructing the use of reason; and in some it grows to a desire of revenge, and a fixed resolution after deliberation to have that desire satisfied. In some anger breaks out into boisterous words, loud menaces, and other inordinate speeches, which are the black smoke whereby the fire of anger and wrath, kindled within, first manifests itself, and then anger proceeds to evil speaking, uttering disgraceful and contumelious speeches, by which the party incensed doth endeavor to stain the reputation of him who hath seemed to have offered him or her a wrong: Of this sort was Saul's anger, 1 Sam. 20.30. Now all and every degree of anger doth grieve the Holy Spirit of God, and darken much the Work of Grace in the heart; there being no sins more opposite to *the fruits of the spirit* mentioned in Gal. 5.22. Then those sins are so, that where such sins are given way, Grace must needs be on the decaying hand. O the prevalence of sinful passion is very injurious to the Spirit of God! it grieves the Spirit so much, that he will withdraw his motions, his guidance, assistance, and comforts from angry persons. *O then, if thou would'st not grieve the Spirit of God, lay aside all bitternesss, wrath, and anger, etc. Consider what an heinous evil anger, wrath, and frowardness of Spirit is. Thou dost not only by thy passion grieve thy Friend or near Relation, but also the Spirit of God: and wilt thou be so ungrateful as to grieve that Spirit that hath done thee so much good, that is appointed by the Father and by Jesus Christ to be thy Comforter, even the Comforter of thy Spirit. If thou hadst an ingenious Spirit, thou would'st think it an ill thing to grieve thy Friend, and if thou hearest thou hast done that which hath grieved him, it will grieve thee exceedingly. O then, how should it trouble thee and grieve thee, that when thou art in an angry passion thou dost grieve the dearest Friend thou hast in the world, thou dost grieve the holy Spirit of God.*

3. O Husband! or O wife! by thy giving way to excessive anger, thou dost *give place to the Devil*, Ephes. 4.27. Thou dost cast open the doors to Satan, the capital enemy of thy Soul, to enter thy heart, and incite thee by his incessant suggestions to act some mischief. As Satan is dethroned and shut out of the hearts of all true believers, and though he shall never reign over them at his pleasure, yet he is daily watching and searching out, if it were but the narrowest passage, and least opportunity, whereby he may again re-enter his old possession, and exercise his former Tyranny: and where excessive or sinful anger is not only given way to, but also continued in, there doth Satan get an open door to settle himself in the heart, and exercise his power, by inciting the person guilty to commit more wickedness. A furious angry person is the prey of Satan: for this raging passion having put out the eye of an angry persons reason, Satan makes him a fit instrument for his own business: so that unadvised anger is a notable means that Satan useth to work some person's destruction; for when once rage hath blinded the eye of reason, he can easily lead a person into a gulf of all wickedness. O then, if thou dost permit anger to rage in thy Spirit, if thou dost nourish thy froward humor, and art so often contending with thy Husband or with thy Wife, thou dost gratify thy self exceedingly, thou dost do as he would have

thee, thou dost give him a welcome entertainment in thy heart. Alas! how canst thou fancy such a monstrous Fiend, as to comply with his suggestions! Be not so vile a wretch, as to be kind to the mortal enemy of thy Soul. His design is to have thee angry, and so contentious, that he may hinder the exercise of thy reason, and so make thee unreasonable in thy actions. O then, when thy anger begins to rise, suppress it with this consideration, *If I give way to my anger, I please no one but the Devil, all others except the Devil are displeased with my anger and frowardness.* That act must needs be dreadfully evil which the Devil doth rejoice in the doing of. What a sad wretch wilt thou evidence thy self to be, in despising the counsel of God, and following the Devils! God bids thee not to be of an hasty spirit, but to forgive the trespasses of thy Brother; and the Devil tells thee, *Be not such a fool as to pass by such wrongs, or suffer such opposition*: and wilt thou slight God, to hearken to the Devil? shall the Devil prevail more with thee than God? Wilt thou shut the door of thy heart against God, and open it to let in Satan? Then thou makest thy self a Child of the Devil, and not a Child of God; and in thy rage and fury dost resemble the Devil, *who goes about like a roaring Lion, seeking whom he may devour.*

4. Persons by their sinful anger, their contentious wrangling and frowardness of spirit, do subject themselves to the wrath of God, and bring his curse upon them; yea, their anger brings upon them even in this life the dreadful effects of God's anger. O thou angry Husband, or angry Wife! if thou dost not repent thee of thy sinful anger, frowardness, hastiness, and touchiness of spirit upon every trivial occasion, God will deal with thee in his anger, as thou would'st deal with thy Husband or Wife in thy anger: for as we forgive others, so doth God forgive us. If therefore thou retain thine anger towards thine Husband, God will retain

his anger towards thee. The Lord acteth the part of an Umpire, to make up breaches, heal differences, and make reconciliation between Relations; but if either of them be so stiff and contentious, that he or she will not be reconciled, what doth that party else, but by froward behavior and obstinate stiffness refusing the Lord's arbitrement and determination, make God his enemy? Eliphaz tells Job, cap. 5.2. *Wrath killeth the foolish man*: That may be taken two ways very true; the wrath of God kills or destroys the wrathful, rash, and inconsiderate man, that hath no true government of himself; for *anger resteth in the bosom of fools,* Eccles. 7.9. or the angry man kills himself; his own wrath is as a Knife to his throat, and as a Sword in his own bowels. Wrath properly is anger inveterate; Wrath is a long anger. When a man or woman is set upon it, when the Spirit is steeped or soaked in anger, then it is wrath: but in this place I conceive it notes a fervent heat, and distemper of Spirit presently breaking forth, or an extreme vexation, fretting or disquieting within, as in Psal. 112.10. *The wicked shall see it, and be grieved*. That is, he shall have secret indignation in himself to see matters go so; he shall gnash with his teeth, and melt away. Gnashing of the teeth is caused by the vexing of the heart, and therefore said *he shall melt away*, which notes an extreme heat within; so that a person's wrath makes him or her melt away, as we say of a person furiously vexed, *it mellows his* (or her) *grease with chafing*. This is an effect of Divine displeasure, whereby God in judgment doth suffer people's wrath to be so vexatious to them, that it makes their lives a continual death to them, and at last so weary and waste their spirits, that they die for very grief; and except the Lord be merciful to them, and the death of Christ heal the wounds that their anger and impatience have made, they will murder their own Souls; for ever frowardness and anger is a person's sin and torment. For *People tear themselves in their anger,*

Job 18.4. The more fretful people are, the more miserable do they make themselves. Those that are of wrathful spirits will certainly feel some degrees of the wrath of God either in this life, or in the life to come. That must needs be hurtful, yea mortal to men, that carries in it a resistance to the immortal God. Some anger is not only grief for the opposition that persons meet with, but a kind of stomaching at God who permits them to be opposed or crossed, and though they do not confess it to be so, yet the spirit of God knows it to be so.

Now know that the wrath of man against man is a sin which God will punish with further wrath. God will pour out wrath upon wrathful persons: and it appears that the wrath of man stirs up God to punish man, if we observe what the Apostle saith in Gal. 5.15. *If ye bite and devour one another*. What is this *biting* and *devouring*? that is, every act which is opposite to that love which God commands us to exercise towards our Neighbor, or our near and dear Relation, is a *biting* and *devouring*. We *bite* and *devour* one another when we are unkind, wrathful and vexatious one to another. See what follows as the effect of their passionate and froward carriages one to another. Take heed ye be not consumed one of another. Take heed lest by walking so unlike Christians, and so unanswerable to the Law of Gospel-love, you provoke God to kindle such a fire among you, and in you, as may prove an utter consumption. When Husbands and Wives are not careful to walk together in love, as Christ hath loved us, God sometimes (as an evidence of his wrath and displeasure) gives them up to a spirit of contention; and their breaches are like the Sea which cannot be healed. Their cruel and harsh dealings (which are yet but to the vexing and healing of one another's spirits, or to devouring and eating one another's credit) may provoke such Judgments as shall destroy their Persons, Families and

Estates, until nothing be left. Thus people's peevish, froward and angry carriages to such as are their nearest Relations, provoke God to execute revenges on them. When an Husband or Wife is fierce towards the other, God is angry with that person, and will not suffer that person to live in peace, who hath so much love to dissention; and this Judgment of God upon persons, is both the forerunner and demonstration of further, yea, the final Judgment: And so saith Solomon, in Prov. 19.19. *A man of great wrath shall suffer punishment.* And Christ denounceth great Judgment against unadvised anger, in Mat. 5.22. *He that is angry with his brother without cause, is in danger of judgment*; intimating, that rash anger is a capital offense, and doth bring a person under the severe sentence of God's Judgment. In the latter part of the verse Christ saith, *That if a person's anger break out in disrespectful speeches the sin is the more capital*, because such an one gives words of disdain. *Whosoever shall say to his brother,* Raca, *shall be in danger of the Council*: but if anger and disdain proceed so far as to reproach a brother yet more despitefully, and call him *Fool*, then that person *shall be in danger of Hell-fire. Consider then, O Husband, or O Wife! the dreadful effects of thine anger, wrath, and frowardness. It subjects thee to the wrath of God, and Oh! what punishments, what consuming judgments doth God's wrath bring forth!* The wrath of God may be specificated into any Judgment, it produceth every evil. If God's wrath be kindled but a little, if it be but as a spark, it will quickly grow up to a flame and consume all, as in Numb. 16.46. Moses bids Aaron haste to make the Atonement, *for* (saith he) *wrath is gone out from the Lord, the Plague is begun.* But know, the wrath of God is not a passion in him, but an action towards man: He acts as men when they are angry, but he suffers nothing by his anger: He smites, and wounds, and pulls down, and destroys, like a wrathful man, yea, an enraged man, yet he doth this in the exactest frame and sweetest composure of his Spirit. But the wrath of God is only his holy and most blessed will burning with hatred against sin, especially the wrath and dissentions of such near Relations as Husband and Wife; and so he turns away from such in his high displeasure. And as the wrath of God draws out punishments, so thy angry, froward, pettish humors, draws out the wrath of God. The wrath of God is terrible, and that must needs be a terrible evil that provokes God to pour it out. Will it not then be grievous to thee to behold the appearances of the wrath of God against thee, and smart under the kindlings of Divine displeasure? O who can abide the coming of the Lord with consuming fire! A fire kindled only to consume, is dreadful, as in Isa. 10.17. *The light of Israel shall be for a fire, and his holy One for a flame, and it shall burn and devour his thorns and his briars in one day.* That is, the fury of the Lord shall appear against those, that like briars and thorns in their anger and contention do prick and scratch one another, though in a strict sense it relates unto God's consuming the Assyrians who plagued the Jews. Should not then the terrible wrath of God (that thy furious spirit brings upon thee) scare thee from cherishing thy passionate and froward humor? If thou retain thine anger against thy Husband or against thy Wife, God will settle his wrath upon thee. O think upon this, O Husband, or O Wife! when thy choler begins to rise, *If I give way to mine anger, I do but call upon God to pour down his wrath upon me.*

Before I proceed to give directions for the subduing, bridling, and preventing wrath and dissention between Husband and Wife, I shall endeavor to manifest which of them is most principally faulty in causing heats and dissentions between them, which of them is most faulty in being angry and froward; and that in these following particulars:

1.

That person that in his or her anger doth by expressions manifest a contempt or undervaluing, or a want of affection to the other's person, is principally faulty in being angry, and is indeed angry immoderately, and without cause; for a well-grounded anger doth manifest displeasure against another's offense and sin, but not against the persons offending, endeavors to make faulty persons *ashamed*, but not a *shame*. That Husband that doth in his anger and furiousness of spirit call his Wife *Whore*, doth indeed evidence a contempt and hatred of her person; and that Wife that doth call her Husband *Rogue, Knave*, and *cheating Fellow*, or other opprobrious terms, doth really hate her Husband, and is principally in fault when a difference doth arise between them. Also that person that doth obstinately refuse to give due conjugal respects to the other, doth evidence a contempt of the other's person, and is guilty of its own anger, and of the strife that is stirred up between them.

2. That party that keeps in memory, and repeateth over old things that have been the occasion of contention a long time before, is guilty of sinful anger, is the promoter of new passions, and is the cause of the present discord; for such a party doth deliberately endeavor to raise new strife and contention: for as for-

mer provocations ought to be forgiven, so they ought to be forgotten. Prov. 17.9. *He that covereth a transgression, seeketh love; but he that repeateth a matter, separateth very friends,* even such near Friends as Husband and Wife: And usually that person that frequently repeateth former transactions, hath a prejudice against the party of whom and to whom he or she repeateth the matter, and by additions and passionate perversions aggravateth the things that are so repeated. So either the Husband or the Wife that makes a fresh rehearsal of old matters, doth but increase his or her own fury, and fully evidence his or her own faultiness.

3. That party that doth in anger upbraid the other with natural Infirmities, or with such failings as he or she was (through the power of temptation) overtaken in, by a surprise, and doth it in a vexatious way to cast a slur or disgrace upon the other, is chiefly faulty in raising discord between them, and is guilty of sinful anger, being the duty of Husband and Wife to forbear everything that may cause any breaches between them.

4. That Wife that doth divulge her Husband's miscarriages to any third person, and talk in company what evil he hath done, is really and principally the kindler of her own causeless anger, and the only occasion of discord between her and her Husband; for that Husband that doth manifest anger against his Wife before others, or that Wife that is discovering her fiery disgust of spirit against her Husband when others are present, that she cares not at what time she vents herself, though it be at such a time that she is like to do no good with it. *This thy violence of passion doth evidence, that thou art the alone cause of thine own anger, because such near Relations are bound not to divulge the dishonorable failings of each other. The Reputation of thy Husband or thy Wife must be as dear to thee as thine own.* It is a sinful and unfaithful practice of many, both Husbands and Wives, who among their Compan-

ions, and also amongst their Servants, are opening the faults and infirmities of each other, which they are bound in tenderness to cover, as if they perceived not that by dishonoring one another they dishonor themselves. They twain being but one flesh, the *dishonor of one* is the *disgrace of the other*. Love will cover a multitude of faults, 1 Pet. 4.8. Nay, many disaffected peevish persons will aggravate one another's faults behind their backs to strangers, and sometimes slander them, and speak more than is truth, and this is the effect of that person's sinful anger and displeasure against the other. Many a man hath been put to it to vindicate himself in a public way, to clear his good name from the slanders of a jealous and passionate Wife. An open enemy is not capable of doing so much wrong to him, as she that is in his bosom, because she is easily to be believed, as being supposed to know him better than any other: therefore that Wife that is not tender of the Reputation of her Husband, but in her anger will speak things before others that tends to his disgrace and reproach is certainly guilty of sinful anger, and the cause of all the discord that is between them.

But perhaps she will say, *My Husband hath spoken words to others in his anger, that tended to my disparagement; and why may not I speak words to others that are dishonourable to him?*

In answer to this, *Know, that the sin of thy Husband cannot justify thine own sin, neither is that a good Argument to justify thy offending God, because thy Husband offended God likewise. It may be thy Husband in his haste did once unadvisedly speak something to thy dishonor, but thou mak'st it a frequent practice upon every slight occasion of thy disgust: Thy Husband may have desisted such a practice, but thou continuest it; and in excuse of the continuance of thy sinful practice in reproaching thy Husband, thou dost upbraid him with that single act of speaking something that was not honorable to thee, which perhaps by thy untoward carriages thou might'st give him great provocations to do. So that notwithstanding all that thou canst plead for thy self, thou art the alone cause of thine own anger, and of all the strife that happens between thy self and Husband.*

5. That party is truly guilty of sinful anger, that takes distaste at every frivolous matter, or anything done unadvisedly, and through indiscretion, which the party offending doth acknowledge; that doth rage for a trifle, or things not worth taking notice of, that are not at all offensive to God, but only not correspondent to his or her corrupt and imperious will. That party that doth this, is the sole cause of all contentions that do arise between them.

6. That party is guilty of sinful anger, that when contentions do arise at any time between Husband and Wife, that doth first of all give railing, reviling, filthy, and reproachful language; for no person's anger can be lawful and holy, that doth not observe Christian modesty in abstaining from malicious and wicked speeches, and unjust and spiteful actions, in expressing his or her anger; for such as justify themselves with spiteful and bitter speeches, are not at all guided by the spirit of God. It is usual when an Husband or Wife is causelessly angry, and cannot convince the other of any particular offense against God, to rail at the other for some contempt that he or she apprehends to have received from the other. And indeed none are more injurious to others, than those who rail at others in reproachful speeches for pretended injuries to have received from others, that reviler's pride hath occasioned his or her own anger, and promoted the discord between them.

7. That party that doth most justify his or her anger, that like Jonah saith, *I do well to be angry*, and will not be convinced of the evil of his or her anger, but will make vain and frivolous pretenses to excuse it, is principally guilty of sinful anger, and is

principal causer of the difference that happens between them, as Husband and Wife.

8. That person, either Husband or Wife, that after some heats and differences between them, is most backward to the performance of Family-worship, and will order, or set about any unnecessary business or lawful employment to interrupt it, is guilty of sinful anger, and the only occasion of difference between them. For whatever a person hath done that indisposeth him or her, or maketh him or her averse to the service of God, is sinful. When the rage of one is grown so high, as not to pray with the other, or join in Sacraments together, at least not willingly, or with complacency, but after hath joined in prayer will quarrel at the matter of Prayer, carp at expressions used in Prayer, and censure the party praying guilty of hypocrisy, or if the party praying vent his own passions in Prayer, that party that is guilty in any of these respects, is guilty of sinful and causeless anger, and was the only cause of the difference that happened between them.

9. That person is the most faulty person, and most guilty to sinful anger, which is not willing to be reconciled again when once displeased, but will retain anger a great while; that person doth manifest much stoutness and proudness of spirit. When vain trifles have stirred up an Husband or Wife to wrath, his or her perseverance in it, doth evidence that it did seem to begin without a cause; and so against all reason the injustice of his or her anger makes him or her to persist in it with the greater obstinacy; and therefore thou dost retain it, yea increase it, because thou may'st not seem to others to be angry without a cause, and that the greatness of thine anger may make others believe that it could not choose but arise from a weighty occasion and just cause, and so thou dost choose rather to *seem* just, than *be* just. But the continuance of anger must needs be sinful, because the

Apostles injunction is, *that we must not let the Sun go down upon our wrath*, Ephes. 4.26. That person that can lie down and sleep, and awake in an angry fit, is very faulty in being angry, and is the principal cause of the difference that is continued between him and his Wife, or her and her Husband.

That party, either Husband or Wife, in whose bosom anger is permitted to rest, *is guilty of the greatest folly*, Eccles. 7.9. That woman that is in a burning feverish fit of anger for a long time, is certainly sinfully angry, because there is a great evil in this abiding of anger. Indeed the longer anger continues, the more it grows, and the longer time anger is drawn out, the greater distance thou wilt be at from thy Husband, with whom thou art angry, and thou art one that delightest to drink of no other waters but of *Massah, Meribah*, of the waters of strife and anger long retained, is in danger of receiving some sourness of malice from the dregs of thy corruption.

The continuance of this inhumane fury hath dissolved even the most sacred friendship upon very frivolous occasions.

I come now to give some Directions for the preventing, moderating, and suppressing angry fits that usually arise between Husband and Wife.

1.

Endeavor in the way of God the mortification of that prevailing principle of flesh that is in thee, if thou would'st be restrained from thy violent passions. So long as the flesh is deeply rooted in thee, it will bring forth its fruits; and anger, wrath, malice and contention are the fruits of the flesh. If thou would'st not have such ill fruits come forth from thy flesh, endeavor always to destroy the root of thy corruptions; for the weaker thy fleshly principle is, the seldomer wilt thou be moved to anger. The mortification of indwelling sin remaining in our mortal bodies, that it may not have life and power to bring forth the deeds and works of the flesh, is the constant duty of believers. Indwelling sin is the same which I mean by a fleshly principle. Now the more powerful thy corruptions are, the more violent will thy passions be, which are the offspring of thy inbred corruption: Thou canst not (while in the body) utterly destroy indwelling sin, that it should have no more hold at all, no residence in thy heart; but this thou must aim at, and earnestly desire: thou must with thy heart really desire that indwelling sin should leave neither root or fruit in thy heart or life. Therefore the mortification that I press thee to set upon, is an habitual weakening of indwelling sin, that thou may'st not be so much under the power of a strong bent and inclination unto sin, that it may not have such life, power, vigor, promptness and readiness to be stirring. This mortification that I here intend, is a daily endeavor after the weakening and abolishing of indwelling sin by little and little, that it might not incline thee and employ thee with such efficacy to make thee a servant to it, as heretofore. If thou let the root of thy corruption abide in strength and vigor, it will be still bringing forth new fruits of the flesh, and thou wilt be hurried into violent passions upon every slight occasion. And if we see persons raging in wrath and fury, we may conclude that indwelling sin is in its full power and vigor in them.

Now, thou canst not carry on this work of Mortification, except thou art engrafted into Christ by Faith. I do not say, Except thou art assured of it, but *Thou must be indeed a true believer*, because mortification is not done without the aid of God's Spirit, who is promised to do it, and all other means are vain without him. Now the Spirit's aid for the work of mortification is not gained except we are in Christ by Faith, and when we are in Christ we have the Spirit, and so have power for mortification. All attempts then for mortification of indwelling sin without an interest in Christ, are vain; for there must be first Conversion and Faith in Christ, then mortification will ensue. Know then, that sin cannot be killed without an interest in the death of Christ, or mortified without the Spirit. Thou then being a believer, make daily and sincere opposition of indwelling sin; rise then mightily against the first movings and acting of thy corruption, against its first conceptions; let it not have allowance from thee for one step, for it is impossible to fix bounds to it. If thou findest thy corruption to begin to entangle thy thoughts, rise up with all thy strength against it, with no less indignation than if it had fully accomplished what it aimed at, else it will get ground in the affections to delight in it; and if thou findest it too powerful an enemy for thee, set Faith on work in Christ for the killing of thy sin. His blood is the great sovereign remedy for sin-sick Souls. Fill thy Soul with the due consideration of that provision which is laid up in Christ for this end, that thy corruptions may be mortified. Behold the Lord Christ that hath all fullness of Grace in his heart, all fullness of Power in his hand: He is able to slay all thy corruptions, there is provision enough in him for thy relief and assistance. Then raise up thy heart by faith to an expectation of relief from Christ, and thy Soul shall be satisfied with the relief it expects, he will assuredly deliver thee, he will slay thy corruptions. Mortification of sin is one peculiar end of the death of Christ, which shall assuredly be accomplished by it. And this whole work that I am pressing thee to endeavor after, is effected, carried on, and accomplished by the power of the Spirit in all the parts and degrees of it; and that thou may'st have more power to oppose and weaken the power of thy corruptions, beg of God earnestly for Christ's sake to give thee his Spirit. O then, is it from the corruption in thy heart that thy passions break out against thy Husband or against thy Wife in thy life? Is it thy corruption that makes thee froward and contentious, that makes discord between thee and thy Husband? Then bend all thy strength against thy corruptions, by the aid of the Spirit endeavor the *mortification of the deeds of the flesh,* Rom. 8.13. Before the strength of thy corruption is weakened, thy anger and frowardness will not be prevented; for as the motions of original sin are permanent, thou wilt not be rid of the body of Death, until the death of thy body; so they are exceeding violent and impetuous in their operations, and puts people into violent passions upon small occasions. If thou dost not oppose thy corruptions, thou dost not endeavor to prevent thy breaking out into furiousness of Spirit. Keep down then thy indwelling sin, and thou wilt not have such hot contests with thy Husband or with thy Wife, for *quarrelling and contention come from the Lusts that are within,* James 4.1. Consider then whenever anything displeaseth thee, *If I be angry, I gratify my corruptions, which I am bound to mortify,* Col. 3.5. Certainly thy froward carriages to thy Husband do arise more from the evil that is within thee than the displeasure that is done thee. Thou hast just cause to say, *It is not my temptation, but my corruption, that makes me froward*; and so do thou fall a studying to mortify thy corruptions if ever thou wilt prevent thy passions.

2. Consider, O Husband, and O Wife! if you will prevent fallings out with one another, keep up your conjugal love in a constant heat and vigor. Love will suppress wrath, as well as prevent it, you cannot have a bitter mind upon small provocations against those that you dearly love, much less can you proceed to reviling words, or to averseness and estrangedness, or any abuse of one another; or if a breach or wound be unhappily made, the balsamic quality of Love will heal it; but when Love once cooleth, small matters will exasperate and breed distaste: Therefore I shall give some directions how conjugal love may be maintained and preserved.

1. Take more notice of the good that is in one another, than the evil. Let not the observation of one another's faults make you overlook or forget one another's Virtues. Love is kindled and preserved by the sight of Love and Goodness. If you will observe nothing in one another but your infirmities, and some indiscreet, inconsiderate, and unadvised actings: You neither preserve Love, nor keep Peace with one another. If you will magnify faults in one another, and slight and despise any good qualities, you take the readiest course to destroy conjugal love, and beget hatred to one another: therefore turn away your eyes from one another's human frailties, and prize what you can see of God in one another, and put a charitable construction upon words and actions; and this is an excellent way to cherish conjugal love, and prevent dissentions between you.

2. Stir up that most in one another into exercises which

are best, and stir not up that which is worst. Avoid that which will move your corruptions to violent operations; use such actions as may provoke one another unto love and good works, and then the good that is in you will most appear, and the evil will be as buried. There is some uncleanness in the best on Earth, and if you will be daily stirring the filth, no wonder if you have the annoyance, and for that you may thank yourselves. Draw out the fragrance of that which is good and delectable in one another, and do not by your imprudence or peevishness stir up the worst, and then you will find that the most faulty of you will appear more amiable to you, and then conjugal love will be increased, and strife prevented.

3. Make not one another froward by froward carriages one to another: behave yourselves to one another in all gentleness and mildness of Spirit. A mild Christian is an healing person, who is skillful to cure the Diseases of the mind, and very instrumental to preserve love and unity. A mild Christian is loving in all carriages, and Love will cause Love as Fire kindleth Fire; and the stronger your love is to one another, the better agreement there will be one with another.

4. *Take much delight in the love, company and converse of each other, this is the way to perpetuate conjugal love to each other; there is nothing that a person's heart is so inordinately set upon as delight, yet the lawful delight allowed them by God they can turn into disdain: the delight that would entangle persons in sin, and turn them from their duty, and from God, is that which is forbidden them, but this is a delight that is helpful to you in your duty, and would keep you from sin. When Husband and Wife take pleasure in one another, it uniteth them in duty, and helpeth them with ease to do the work that relates to each other, and bear their burdens. Avoid therefore all things that may represent you unpleasant and unlovely to each other, and use all lawful means to cherish complacency*

and delight. All unseemly carriage and foolish speech which savor of contempt must be shunned, as temptations which would hinder you from that love, pleasure and content which Husband and Wife should have in one another. This is the way to preserve conjugal love, and restrain from anger.

5. *To preserve conjugal love between each other, be faithful in rendering all due conjugal respects to each other, that the ends of lawful marriage may not be neglected: The neglect of those duties, as it is a sin forbidden of God, so it breeds a contempt of each other, as it may be a means of provoking one another to sin, so it doth abundantly destroy love to each other. Read what the Apostle saith in* 1 Cor. 7.1-5. It is good for a man not to touch a woman; nevertheless, to avoid fornication, let every man have his own Wife, and every Woman her own Husband. Let the Husband render unto the Wife due benevolence, and likewise also the Wife unto the Husband. The Wife hath not power over her own body, but the Husband: likewise also the Husband hath not power over his own body, but the Wife. *Defraud you not one another, except it be with consent for a time, that ye may give yourselves to Fasting and Prayer, and come together again, that Satan tempt you not for your incontinence.* Therefore those persons live contrary to the nature of their Relation, who withdraw from one another in this respect: and a faithful discharge of these conjugal duties, doth very much establish love to each other, and very much prevent anger and discord.

6. *Beware you do not neglect the worship of God in your families, for if in your families you give not God so much service as he requires, he will permit you to withdraw respects from each other; and this God will do, because you neglect to pay the respects that you owe to him. Faithfulness and delight in God's service is the way to make you faithful to, and to delight in each other. When*

any breaches do arise between you, consider whether you have not neglected Family-worship, for God expects if you will have him bless you with a permanent love to each other, that you and your house do serve him. This is the way to procure God's blessing on you and yours, and preserve peace and constant friendship between you, and to restrain you from doing anything in passion, roughness, and sourness of spirit.

7. If thou art an Husband that readest this subject, do thou so unite authority and love, that neither of them be omitted or concealed, but let both be exercised and maintained. Love must not be exercised so imprudently, as to destroy the exercise of Authority; and Authority must not be exercised so mysteriously, as to destroy the exercise of Love. As thy Love must be a governing Love, so thy Commands must be all loving Commands. Lose not thy Authority, for that will but disable thee from doing the office of an Husband to a Wife, or of a Master to thy Servants: yet it must not be maintained by fierceness and cruelty, because not consistent with conjugal love. For there is no case of inequality so great, in which conjugal Love is not to be exercised. Observe but this rule, and Love will grow exceedingly between thee and thy Wife.

8. If thou art a Wife, and would'st preserve fervent conjugal love between thee and thy Husband, live in a voluntary obedience and subjection to him, 1 Pet. 3.1. Col. 3.18. Ephes. 5.22. If his softness or yieldingness cause him to relinquish his Authority, and for peace he is fain to let thee have thy will, yet remember that it is God that hath appointed him to be thy Head and Governor; and thou having chosen him as such, thou must carry it towards him in a submissive, and not in a ruling and masterly way, and do not deceive thy self to think it enough to give the bare title of Government to thy Husband, when yet thou wilt in all things have thine own will, for this is but mockery, and not obedience; and self-willedness is contrary to subjection and obedience. Now a neglect of giving due subjection to thy Husband, and thy usurping authority over him, and behaving thy self insolently and imperiously towards him, doth cause conjugal love to decay, and cause a breach of friendship and peace between thee and thy Husband. But an humble, submissive and obedient carriage of thy self to thy Husband, doth increase love between you, and keep you both in a moderate, calm and quiet frame of spirit.

9. *As thou art a Wife, so honor thy Husband according to his superiority, behave not thy self towards him with irreverence and contempt in titles, speeches, or behavior. If the worth of his person deserveth not Honor, yet his place deserves it,* Ephes. 5.33. *And the Wife see that she reverence her Husband; that is, that she inwardly acknowledge that degree of Honor which God hath put upon him,* 1 Cor. 11.3. *and give evident testimonies of thy inward esteem in words, actions, and whole carriage,* 1 Pet 3.6. *especially in thy loathness to offend him. That Wife that cares not what contempt she casts upon her Husband, will not preserve conjugal love long. Nothing more distastes an Husband, than to be slighted and despised by one that is bound to honor and reverence him: Indeed it begets great distractions between them: But if thou desirest a continuation of conjugal love, if ever thou desirest to prevent anger and furious passion in thy self or Husband, and as ever thou desirest peace to be kept between thy self and Husband, do not affront him with contempt of his superiority.*

10. *As thou art a Wife, if thou hast a desire to maintain conjugal love between thy self and Husband, and prevent discord between you, then live in a cheerful contentedness with thy condition, take heed of a froward, impatient, and murmuring spirit. It is a continual burden to a man to have an impatient and discontented Wife. Many a man can bear great afflictions, that yet is not*

able to bear his Wife's impatience. It must needs trouble him to hear his Wife vexing, fretting, and murmuring at the Works and Providences of God; to hear her night and day complaining and speaking distrustfully, and to see her live disquietly, is far heavier than any affliction; for thereby she refuseth to submit to the will of God, and is not willing that God should choose her conditions for her, but is dissatisfied with God's dealings with her. O then! as thou desirest to prevent the decay of conjugal love, if thou wilt prevent the disturbing thy self with angry passions, as thou desirest to live in peace and quietness, strive to keep a cheerful spirit under all thy disappointments, submit to the will of God under all his dispensations, beware of muttering, and manifesting discontent when God's Providences do not suit thy humor. Thus thou seest the way to preserve conjugal love. Follow those directions, that you may walk sweetly and lovingly together. If you had more love one to another, you would have less discord between one another, and you would not be so soon angry one with another. Where passion is violent, love is weak. Were your love stronger, your angry passions would be weaker. You cannot carry it frowardly to one whom you dearly love. You can have but little esteem of that person that you are angry with upon every trifle. Indeed that woman that carries it imperiously and furiously towards her Husband, had never any real love for him, she married him before she loved him. O then! put an high price upon the quietness of your spirits, and be not easily deprived of the sweetness of it. Do not let your frowardness, caused by a defect of love to each other, destroy your calmness and serenity of spirit for a trifle. Where conjugal love is defective, the Husband and Wife never knew what the sweetness of a quiet, meek and patient spirit meant. O then! keep warm your conjugal love, that will make you prize a quiet spirit at an high rate, and be willing to suffer much for it, and follow after it, because there is so much good in it. Love will make great crosses and provocations easy to be born. Do then nothing that may occasion a decay of love between you.

3. If you would prevent the occasions of wrath and discord, you must mortify your pride, which is the cause of anger and impatience. A proud and contentious spirit always go together. You that are Wives are most subject to this sin. Your Pride will make you turbulent and unquiet with your Husbands, and contentious with all your Neighbors. Your frowardness, anger and discontent, are the only effects of the height of your Spirits. Except you can (as the Apostle adviseth, Col. 3.12.) *put on humbleness of mind, you will never have meekness of spirit*: for proud spirits are usually fiery spirits; but humility is patient, and doth not aggravate injuries. If then you would keep a quiet frame of Spirit, free from anger and impatience, be sure that you keep an humbled Soul, that over-valueth not itself. Such as think meanly of themselves, think meanly of all that is said or done against them; but such as magnify themselves, do magnify their Provocations. Pride is the most impatient sin; it is the Devil's bellows to kindle people's corruptions, and set the hearts of near Relations and whole Families in a flame: for that without mortifying of Pride there is no possibility of preventing anger, impatience, and hot contests between Husband and Wife. That party that is proud will take everything amiss that is spoken or done by the other. 'Tis humbleness of mind in Husband or Wife that will keep all things quiet between them: therefore I shall endeavor to give some Directions to help you to mortify the pride of your hearts.

1. Labor to set the excellency of the grace of Humility before your Souls, and meditate on the beauty and excellency of this Grace, and by being convinced of the excellency of this grace, you will abhor the pride of your hearts, and come to be adorned with humility. None so submissive to the will of God; none so

contented in the condition that God puts them; none so prevalent in Prayer, none so quiet, and free from disturbances; none so serviceable to God; none receive more grace and favor from God, than humble Souls: None do more patiently bear crosses, and imitate Christ, than humble Souls: None so thankful for mercies as such as are sensible of their unworthiness of mercies. O how beautiful doth humility make a Soul! O then, how desirous should all be to be clothed with humility! This would preserve peace and unity, and endear love between Husband and Wife. For this would prevent your giving offense to each other, or taking offense at each other. If you were convinced of the excellency of this grace, you would be fond of no other excellency, you would not think better of yourselves than others, you would not boast of what you have, but be humbled for what you want. If you did not over-value yourselves for some seeming worth or excellency that you apprehend to be in you, you would not so much storm at everything that opposeth you.

2. Press much after a clearer knowledge and fuller discovery of God. The more you do converse with God, the more humble you will be, and the more will the pride of your hearts be mortified. If you consider God's infinite glorious perfections, and the immensity and infinite greatness of God, what a distance there is between God and You, it must needs make you have a mean esteem of yourselves. When you compare yourselves with God, you are nothing, yea, less than nothing. Did you see more of the power, more of the sovereignty, more of the holiness of God in Himself, and more of his goodness to You, you would have no heart to exalt yourself, but rather abhor yourselves. The Prophet Isaiah, cap. 6.5. cries out, *He was undone, because such a polluted creature as he was had seen the King, the Lord of Hosts*: His bodily eyes had seen the signs of his presence, and the eyes of his Soul

were so over-pressed with the present weight of his Glory, that in this his frail condition he could not bear it, but cries out, *He was undone*. As he had never seen so much of God before, so he was never so deeply humbled before; he never cried out before, *I am undone*; which word implieth the greatest sense of his own vileness, nothingness, and wretchedness. The true reason why people at any time carry it so high with God, that they have a good opinion of themselves, is, because their notions and apprehensions of God are so infinitely below him. Did they know God more, how would they fear before him, and stand as persons astonished at the presence of his Majesty! It is people's darkness about God which emboldens them beyond their bounds, or the line of Creatures: and the reason why carnal persons and hypocrites carry it so stoutly before God, is, because they know not God aright; *They may boast of their knowledge, when they know nothing as they ought*, 1 Cor. 8.2. Persons never see how imperfect they are, till they see themselves in the light of God's Perfection: when they duly see themselves in that Glass, they greatly abhor themselves, because they see no beauty nor comeliness in themselves, for they cannot but see much deformity in themselves, when they behold the Beauty and Glory of God. As when we behold that Beauty, we shall abhor ourselves for our deformities and defilements, so we shall be daily mending and cleansing ourselves from them. That sight of God Job had, cap. 42.5, 6. humbled him so deeply, as to work in himself abhorrence: *But now mine eye seeth thee, wherefore I abhor my self.*

  1. An abhorrence of a sinful self, or loathing of self for sin and evil done, Ezek. 36.31.

  2. It signifies an abhorrence of righteous self, or a loathing ourselves in the good, yea, even in the best that we have done, Isa. 64.6. So that a truly humble Soul abhorreth his righteousness,

as never to trust in it at all. This the Apostle saith, Philip. 3.7, 8 Self-righteousness is Gold, and to be embraced in conversation; but it is Dung, and to be abhorred in justification. An humble Soul doth abhor self-righteousness, because he is convinced that self-righteousness is a weak and imperfect thing even in sanctification: therefore he is so far from boasting of it, or trusting to it, that he hath a kind of abhorrence of it, that as to justification he looks on it as abominable. And as he abhors it because 'tis unfit and incompetent in itself for justification, so also because it is utterly inconsistent with the tenor of the Gospel, wherein God hath removed all man's Righteousness, how pure soever it may be, from that use, and directed us to look only to the Righteousness of Christ for that use, which the Apostle calls, the *Righteousness of God*, Rom. 10.3. because 'tis that which the Wisdom of God the Father hath provided for us, and which the Worthiness of God the Son hath wrought and procured for us. Pardon this digression, I have reason for what I do. O then! would you get your pride mortified, that begets and feeds your angry passions? endeavor after fuller manifestations of God, seriously consider God as revealed in his Word, converse more with God, get more acquaintance with God, know and consider how much God is above, and the meaner you will be in your own eyes, the fuller discoveries you have of God, the more sensible you will be of your own unworthiness, and the more calmness will you have in your own spirits, and the more able you will be to resist provocations unto anger. We have no cause to wonder to see persons in the world that do not know God, to have bold and presumptuous spirits, and have their spirits lifted up in vanity. But it is a wonder that a Soul that ever had any sight of God should have any rising of spirit, that any sinful heights of spirit should be in that Soul that knows what an infinite God he is to deal with. O converse much with God, and then you will be humble Souls! That Soul that never goes from duty without experiencing communion with God, is very humble, and nothing hath that excellency in it, as that which comes from conversing with God, and upon the sight of his excellency.

3. Consider that the more you see and know yourselves, the more you shall be abased, and lie low in yourselves. A right knowledge of yourselves is that which should bring your hearts low. Do but seriously consider what you are in yourselves, what abundance of filth and vileness there is in yourselves, and you will not have any high thoughts of yourselves. O then study yourselves more, converse with yourselves, and endeavor to know yourselves more, and that noxious wind of ostentation by which proud persons are vainly puffed up in their fleshly minds, will be let out and avoided. Let every proud person consider what he is, let the question be put to his or her own Soul thus. *Who am I? or what am I, that I should have a proud thought? shall dust and ashes, shall one that is but a shadow, a vapor, but as grass, a flower of the field, and in his best estate altogether vanity, be proud? O consider, whatever thou art as to this world, thou canst not be long what thou art; in thy highest perfections attainable in this world, thou art very mutable, and the higher thou art, the more mutable thou art, and what hast thou to be proud of? Shall perishing things be proud things? wilt thou be lifted up with what thou hast, which as to the world, is of so little being, as thou canst hardly be said to be?* Consider all these things, which are as fuel and occasions of thy pride: Thou must shortly give an account for them to God, and the more thou hast received in any kind whatsoever, the stricter will thy account be, for thy *Account* will be proportionable to what thy *Receipt* is. Luke 12.48. T*o whomsoever much is given, of him shall much be required.* Consider what thou art by Nature, and whiles in thy unconverted state thou wert a Child of Wrath, as bad as

the basest and vilest wretch in the world, thou wert full of sin, the seeds of all kind of sin; there is no sin in Hell itself, but the seeds of it were in thy heart; thy heart and life was full of sin, all the faculties of thy Soul were full of sin, all the members of thy body were instruments of sin, thy Soul and Body was polluted and loathsome, and in that condition thou wert succorless and helpless; thou could'st never deliver thy self, thou wert wandering from God, and would'st have wandered eternally, if God had not looked upon thee in mercy: There was such a breach made between God and thy Soul that had all the Angels in Heaven, or Creatures in the world, laid down their lives for thee, thou could'st not by their deaths have helped to make up that breach. Look back to this condition, and thou wilt see cause enough to be low in thine own eyes. Consider what thou might'st now have been, if the Lord had taken advantage against thee: Thou art now in a comfortable condition, thou now comest among the people of God into the assemblies of the Saints, but thou might'st have been amongst the damn'd Reprobates, thou might'st have been roaring in Hell, and sweltering under the wrath of the infinite God, and if God hath made any change in thy state, consider what trouble it put Heaven and Earth unto, that the Son of God must take thy nature upon him, and die, and be made a Curse, to deliver thee from that condition. Now these things should be mighty humbling considerations. Also consider what thou should'st be if God should leave thee, tho' he hath done great things for thee, showed thee himself, Christ, the evil of sin, and, the excellency of eternal life, yet, for all this, if God should but leave thee to thy self for one quarter of an hour, Oh! if God should but withdraw his Spirit from thee one moment, thou would'st depart from him, and lose all that thou hast, and be brought into as miserable a condition as ever thou wert, thou would'st be plunged into the depth of all evil. O certainly serious considerations of these things will very much subdue the pride of thy heart, and keep down the risings of thy Spirit! O then in the midst of thy *fullness* do thou think of thy *emptiness*, and in the midst of thy *perfections* think of thy *deficiencies*. Think how much, and in how many things, thou art wanting, when any thought of Pride ariseth, concerning what thou dost enjoy, and wherein thou dost abound. Indeed thy wantings being a great deal more than thy aboundings, and thy imperfections more than thy perfections, should be to thee a greater matter of humbling, than thy abounding or perfection can be an occasion of Pride. Consider the deficiencies in thy self, how low thou art in knowledge, how low in grace, how much thou art behind others, how much thou art below what thou might'st be; and have attained to, both in the light of Knowledge, and in the strength of Grace, and this will mightily humble thee; then consider how much thou comest short of what others have attained; as it is an excellent means to keep thy Soul from murmuring and discontent, to consider how many are below thee in the enjoyments of the comforts of this life, so it is an excellent means to keep thee from pride to consider how many others are above thee in spiritual endowments so far above thee, as thy knowledge is but ignorance compared with their knowledge, thy strength weakness, thy faith unbelief, thy patience unquietness of spirit, thy very fruitfulness barrenness compared with theirs. Such considerations are mighty humbling considerations. Again, consider and reflect upon thine own sinfulness. Thy defects in good may keep thy heart low, but thy abundance of sinful evils may keep it much lower. Thou hast yet a body of sin and death, that thou carriest about with thee. O abundance of sin and corruption remains in thy Soul! Then consider thy sin as acted and brought forth by thee, consider thy unthankfulness to God, and all thy unworthy walkings before God, notwithstanding what he hath done for thee. Look on sin, and thy heart must needs come down. The remembrance of sin abiding in thee, and acted by thee, is an excellent means to put a stop to the further actings, as of all other sins, so of this sin of Pride also. The reason why thou art so proud of thy self, is, because thou art so ignorant of thy self. Didst thou know thine own ignorance and misunderstandings, didst thou know all those abominations that are in thy heart, what earthly-mindedness, what inordinate Creature-love, what passions, what envy lie there; didst thou know how deceitful and false thy heart is towards God, thy self, and others, such knowledge would make thee strike sail, and come lower, and make thee abhor thy self exceedingly: Didst thou once know thy self aright, what a frail, blind, and sinful Creature thou art, how humble and heavenly would'st thou be! Didst thou rightly know that thou art a Creature, it would cause thee to live more like a new Creature. Didst thou remember that thou art but a Creature, the work of God's hand, this would keep thee low and humble; but didst thou know what a sinful polluted Creature thou art, thou would'st soon come not only to a lower estimate, but an utter abhorrence of thy self. Thou dost over-think thy self, because thou dost not know thy self: Thou dost over-rate thy self, because thou dost not rightly understand thy self. O then, endeavor to understand thy self better; and endeavor to make use of those considerations that I have here hinted. This is the way to make thee sensible of thine own nothingness: This is the way to mortify thy pride, and keep thee humble; and if thou wert more humble, thou would'st be more peaceable with thy Wife or Husband.

  4. Be much in the meditation of Christ's humbling and abasing himself for thee. What can kill pride, if the humblings of Christ do not? How may'st thou school and chastise thy proud Soul with the remembrance of Christ in his abasements! *What!*

was Christ an humble Christ, and shall I be a proud Christian? was he an humble Master, and shall I be a proud Disciple? Did Christ empty himself, and make himself of no Reputation, and shall I, that am but emptiness, be lifted up with a Reputation of myself, or with a Reputation that others have of me? Did Christ abuse himself to the form of a Servant, and shall I lift up myself as if I did reign as a King? Christ humbled himself, and became obedient to death, even the death of the Cross, and what have I to glory in but the Cross of Christ? Gal. 6.14. O then, if thou hast anything to be proud of, 'tis the Cross of Christ. Think then often and much of the humblings of Christ, and then thou wilt think of thy self as a mere nothing: This is the most effectual means through the Spirit to bring down the swellings of thy heart, and to make thee truly humble. And thus I have ended what I have to say in directing thee how to get thy pride mortified and thy spirit humbled. O then, if thou would'st be restrained from sinful anger, and if ever thou would'st have any quiet in thine own spirit, and carry it peaceably and quietly to thy Husband or to thy Wife, endeavor to be of a more lowly spirit, and to be clothed with humility. As long as thou dost nourish thy proud humor, thou wilt fall out with thy nearest Relation for every trifle, but a lowly spirit doth its utmost to preserve peace and unity. Such a one is so tender of others, as that he or she is not willing to grieve anyone in the world, much less an Husband or a Wife. Therefore the Apostle saith, Philip. 2.3. *Let nothing be done through strife and vain-glory, but in lowliness of mind let each esteem others better than themselves.* The lust of vain-glory, whereby a person endeavors more to gain esteem from men, than to honor God, is the mother of contention and strife, and a great enemy to union and peace; and here the Apostle prescribeth *humility* as an Antidote against strife and contention, and a sovereign mean for attaining unto and entertaining of union and peace. But where pride is predominant, men and women walk so, as that they care not to give content to anybody but themselves in the Family; they must have all the content, and nobody else be pleased. Certainly an humble Spirit is much freer from angry passions than any other, because as an humble person is not willing to give offense to any, so is not ready to take offense from others: for it is pride of spirit to be ready to take offense from others upon every trifle, and by this means persons prove to be very burdensome to others. The ground of a proud persons taking offense is this, because they think that everybody must say as they say, and do as they do, else they cry out that they are always opposed, and because they think their own judgments best, and such a thing is better, therefore others must do it, and if they do not, then they are lofty, then they are proud and stout, and break out into unseemly speeches, be inflamed with passion, evidencing that they are under the tyranny of their pride. So that there is no preventing of anger and contention between Husband and Wife, without the mortification of their Pride.

5. Another direction to prevent sinful anger and hot contests between Husband and Wife, is, that thou dost consider that *God is merciful and gracious, slow to anger, and abundant in kindness*, Exod. 34.6. And as he is not easily provoked to anger, so being provoked, his anger lasteth not long; *for he will not always chide, nor keep his anger for ever*, Psal. 103. 8, 9. The Lord with much lenity suffereth the vessels ordained to destruction: how long did he suffer the old world! how loath was he to strike! if in an hundred and twenty years he could have reclaimed them, he would have forborn them, 1 Pet. 3.20. The measure of his grace and mercy towards us is daily, boundless, and exceeding all measure: He forgiveth us every moment much more than we can possibly be wronged of men; yea, he forgiveth that person that

injureth us, much more than we can forgive him. O then, if thou wilt evidence thy self to be a Child of God, must thou not labor to express his Virtues? This is that the Apostle exhorts, Col. 3.12, 13. *Put on therefore as the elect of God, holy and beloved, bowels of mercy, kindness, humbleness of mind, meekness, long-suffering, forbearing one another: If any man have a quarrel against any, even as Christ forgave you, even so do ye.* He recommendeth the practice of meekness and long-suffering; which consists in bearing with, and pardoning of even real injuries done by others, and persuadeth to it from Christ's example in pardoning us. The example of God and Christ is a most convincing pattern for exciting us to pardon and forgive one another, if we consider either the greatness of those wrongs which he pardoneth, Isa. 1.18. or our baseness who do injure him, Isa. 40.17, 22. or his omnipotentcy to right himself of the wrongs done unto him, Mat. 10.28. *Dost thou, O Husband, or O Wife, stand in need of forgiveness, and wilt thou not forgive thy Husband or thy Wife? shall God forgive thee infinite sins, and wilt thou not pass by one offense? dost thou stand in need of a sea of mercy for the washing away thy many foul offenses, and wilt thou not let one drop fall upon thy Husband or thy Wife, to forbear or forgive in trifling wrongs? Certainly if Husbands and Wives would but seriously consider these things, it would make all quarrellings and contentions between them to cease. O what little cause hast thou then to manifest a furious spirit against thy Husband or thy Wife for every trifle, seeing God doth not deal furiously with thee for great offenses! O that these considerations might prevent Husbands and Wives raging against, and falling out one with another for the time to come!*

6. If thou would'st keep thy spirit quiet, and free from furious passions, when anything is done by thy Husband or thy Wife that is contrary to thy mind, and doth much displease, look up to

the hand of God, and acknowledge the Providence of God, without which not the least grief or injury could befall thee; for even the least is a portion of that Cup which the hand of God reacheth out to thee to drink of. Job looked not at the Sabeans and Thieves that took away his Goods, but at the hand of God: *The Lord hath taken away, blessed be his name,* Job 1.21, 22. He was satisfied that God willed that in righteousness and justice, which they acted with so much cruelty and injustice. David's looking up to God when Shimei cursed him, quieted his spirit, and restrained his anger. So in Psal. 39.9. *I was dumb, and opened not my mouth, O Lord, because thou didst it.* He doth neither manifest forwardness nor discontent, because he took notice of the hand of God. Joseph did not vent his passion against his Brethren for selling him to the Ishmaelites, but kept himself in a calm frame of spirit, by considering this, *it was God that sent me hither*. A godly man cannot be angry at the doing or speaking of that which pleaseth God to order the speaking or doing of, because he knows he is bound to submit to the will of God. And thy only observing of the person that doth in any way displease thee, and not considering that God hath an hand in all things that befall thee, is the cause that thou art so often transported with furious passions. An observation that God hath an hand in all things that befall thee, is as water to quench the inflammation of thy angry passions. This persuasion, *That God seeth cause for all the wrongs that thou dost suffer*, is many ways forceable to move thee unto patience. For, 1. *If thou dost look to the hand of God in those things that distaste thee, it will constrain thee to confess that all thy chastisements are just, far less than thy sins have deserved; for indeed all the opposition that thou hast from thy Husband or thy Wife, is in some measure a rebuke of God against some miscarriage of thine. And God in permitting thee to be exercised with such things as do very much distaste thy spirit, doth do thee no wrong, because 'tis not commensurate to the merit of thy sin. For indeed such crosses and provocations as thou dost meet with from thy Husband or thy Wife, are but light to a gracious heart; and if not so light to thee as to others, yet but momentary: but thy sins have deserved infinite and eternal punishments. If therefore the Lord use those earthly rods to correct thy sins, thou should'st rather admire his mercy, than be angry at so gentle chastisements. If thou didst but consider, that the hand of God is in everything whereby thy Husband or thy Wife displeaseth thee, thou would'st see that the manner of the Lord's dealing with thee is tender and compassionate.* Psal. 25.10. All the ways of the Lord are Mercy and Truth, to them that fear him, and keep his Testimonies. *When thou deservest to be cut down root and branch, and cast into unquenchable fire, he doth only lop and prune thee, to make thee more fruitful: Therefore, if the matter be well weighed, thou hast more cause to be thankful, than to be offended. Consider with thy self, when any word is spoken, or any act done, by thy Husband, or by thy Wife, that hath a tendency to discompose thee, and say,* It is the will of God to afflict me in my Wife, or in my Husband: O but this is not the full desert of my sin, this is not Hell, I deserve severer dealings from God than these, a*nd this will suppress thine anger that it break not out.* 3. *Consider when thou dost meet with any matter of provocation from thy Husband or thy Wife, that God in his infinite Wisdom will dispose of everything for thy good, if thou dost love God.* Rom. 8.28. *Why then should'st thou vex thy self with anger, seeing God will turn the injuries, wrongs, crossings, and slightings of thy Husband or thy Wife into blessings. Therefore when any wrong is offered thee which thou canst not by any just and lawful means avoid. Do thou say with our Savior Christ,* John 18.11. Should I not drink of the Cup that my Father hath provided for me? should I be angry with the Cup, because the Physic is bitter; or with the hand whereby it is conveyed to me? My Heavenly Father correcteth me for my good and amendment, I will not therefore be angry with whom I am beaten, but rather look to the principal hand that layeth the chastisement upon me, and the happy fruit that brings with it; a*nd thus thou may'st keep down the risings of thine anger, when thy Husband or thy Wife, doth distaste thee.* 1. If thou didst observe the hand of God in any contradiction that thou hast from thy Husband or Wife, which might make thee angry, thou would'st acknowledge that the present course that God takes with thee to be best; for that is always best, which is ordered by God, who is infinitely good, and in all his dispensations is communicating of some good one way or other to his Creatures. As God is most wise, so his prescriptions are most safe and healthful. Now, (2.) there is good cause why thou should'st cease to be angry for crosses, wrongs and injuries, for otherwise thou wilt be angry with God's disposing of his Providences, resist thine own profit, and choose rather to please thy palate, though to thy greater torment afterwards, than to preserve thy health and peace. O then say to thy self, *Hath God an hand in permitting my Wife to show me such disrespect, or in permitting my Husband to be unkind to me? Is it then my fretting or raging against my Husband or my Wife, an evidence that I am displeased with God for permitting such an act.* When thou art vexed that thou art related to such an one as an Husband, thou art offended with God's appointment. And when thou dost wish that thou hadst never been related to him as thy Husband, thou dost in truth desire God to break thy Relation to him by his death: but know that God seldom gratifies the desires of such humorsome persons, and commonly those that long for the death of another, do die first themselves. Such considerations as these well settled on thy heart, cannot but quiet and pacify thy Soul in the midst of manifold provocations.

6. If thou would'st keep peace and amity between thy self and Husband, or between thy self and Wife, turn thine anger upon thy self; not to tear thy self, but to consider and reprove thy self for thine own miscarriages: a just indignation against the sin of thine own Soul restraineth carnal anger from breaking forth against another: For whosoever is zealous against the errors and disorders of his or her own life, shall not find time to jar and contend with others for petty injuries and wrongs. Experience showeth, that the greatest heat abroad is accompanied with the least at home. A true sight of thine own faults will show thee so much cause to be displeased with thy self, that thou wilt have little leisure, and less cause, to be displeased with thy Husband or with thy Wife. Thou think'st thy self ill dealt with by thy Husband, but if thou considerest thine own sins, thou wilt find that thou hast dealt worse with God, than thy Husband hath dealt with thee; and this is an excellent means to prevent thy being angry with thy Husband, and make thee angry with thy self. *My Husband hath offended me, and I have offended God; God forbears manifesting anger against me, and why should not I forbear mine anger against my Husband?* O then, when thou hast received any seeming injuries from thy Husband before thou dost let forth thine anger against him, ask thine own conscience, *Am I clear from offering the like injuries, or greater, to my Husband? and how many times have I offended God much more?* If thou would'st thus speak to thine own conscience in the presence of God, thou would'st not be so easily incited to anger, seeing thou thy self dost many things that need pardon. And thy greater faults might serve to excuse those that are less in thy Husband, if thou would'st but look upon them: for thou could'st not without blushing be angry with those faults in thy Husband, for which thou shalt need to crave pardon thy self. If thou didst truly judge that by thy sins committed against God,

thou hast deserved not only contumelies and wrongs, but also the eternal death of thy Body and Soul, thou could'st not be easily provoked to anger upon every trifling occasion, nor think it any great disparagement to endure lesser injuries, seeing thou hast deserved greater.

7. If thou would'st suppress thine anger, and live in a sweet harmony and peace with thy Husband or with thy Wife, endeavor to get thy heart more desirous of, and affected with spiritual and heavenly things, that thou may'st have thy conversation in Heaven, and have thy heart always in a spiritual frame. Such a conversation, and such a frame of spirit, will make thee tread under-feet all vain and transitory things, which concern this life, because the Treasures that the Faith of an heavenly Christian discovers, are more excellent and durable than anything this world affordeth: the preferment it longeth after, is not of an earthly nature; the riches it coveteth, are above, as for the things of this life, an heavenly Christian doth not desire much, delighteth not in much, and consequently is not much disturbed with unquietness, nor incensed with anger when crossed in them, for by living in Heaven by Faith, a person's spirit is well ballasted, and made steady, and Heaven is above all storms and tempests, and the more thou dost converse there, the less stormy is thy heart; thou would'st not then trouble thy self needlessly, or be concerned for every domestic trifle, and if anything miscarry thou wilt not so much look to the means, as to the supreme cause, the Providence of God: O, if thou wert an heavenly Christian, thou would'st be lifted up far above these sublunary things, and would'st not be afflicted when crossed in them. Consider then when thou art jarring and contending with thy Husband or with thy Wife, when thou art venting thy self in passion for every trifle, for every unadvised word, for every unsuitable gesture, or for things that are no way sinful, thou dost

evidence that thou art a stranger to an heavenly frame, thy heart is drossy and earthly, thy heart is too much set upon the pleasing of thy humor, and dost prefer thine own will before God's will. If thou would'st be more free from disturbances of spirit by earthly things, and by the carriages of thy Husband or Wife, be more in the contemplation of heavenly things, than in the vanity and emptiness of earthly things, and then thou wilt not think it much to be crossed in things that are of so little worth, and in things that thou dost so little value. Why art thou so much for the pleasing thy self in the things of this life? wilt thou be contented with such things for thy portion? If thou dost look for an Inheritance in Heaven, do not disquiet thy self with every trifle that thou dost meet with in thy way thither. If thou dost think to enter into the Kingdom of Heaven without passing through many tribulations, thou art mistaken: Do not then vex thy self with those things that are usual attendants of a journey to Heaven. Consider with thy self thus; *Why shall I fret my self with a little opposition, or contradiction from my Husband or Wife now? It will not be long before I come home to my Father's house, where I shall be above all opposition; and shall not I bear a little disquiet for an eternal rest?* O! wert thou an heavenly Christian, thou would'st live in more sweetness, amity, content, and satisfaction with thy Husband or with thy Wife.

    8. If thou would'st keep down the risings of thine anger against thy Husband or thy Wife, be exceedingly humbled for thy former breakings out into anger. They that resolve to set upon a duty, and are not humbled for their former neglect of it, are like to do little good by their resolutions: Physicians used to purge out choler by bitter things, and those that would tame wild Creatures keep them in the dark: So humiliation for the distemper of passion is a special means to purge out passion, and to tame and quiet the Spirits of men and women. It may be thou hast been overcome

with passion in froward fits, and thou hast seen the inconvenience of them, and it may be afterwards thou hadst thoughts, O, this is ill, and thou hop'st thou shalt do so no more: But although thou think'st that thou wilt do so no more, yet except thou be humbled for what thou hast done, thou wilt fall to it again upon the next occasion. O then, thou that art often and soon angry with thy Husband or thy Wife for trifles, I appeal to thy conscience, Canst thou affirm that thou hast been under deep humiliation for thy former passions? hast thou smarted in spirit for thy former anger? hast thou mourn'd and been afflicted for thy former hastiness of spirit, and causeless ventings of thy passion? what canst thou answer to this question? O never expect to be restrained from future miscarriages, except thou art truly humbled for former miscarriages of this nature. O therefore, thou that hast such a froward spirit, O get alone, and apply the salt tear of humiliation unto the choler of thy heart, and see what this will do. Humiliation for that which is past, will be a special help to keep thee from barking, snarling at, and biting thy Husband or thy Wife. I use such expressions, because angry persons are very dogged in their carriages one to another.

9. If thou would'st live in peace and quietness with thy Husband or thy Wife, thou should'st be offended with nothing in thy Husband or in thy Wife, but what God is offended with. Such of thy Husband's actions as do displease God, should displease thee. What authority or right hast thou to be offended with thy Husband, when God is not? or what reason canst give why thou should'st be distasted with any of his actions that God is not? Yea, certainly thou ought'st not to find fault with that in thy Husband, which God doth not. If you would both of you more faithfully endeavor to conform to God's will, your wills would be more united, and there would not be such differences between you. But if your

wills do oppose God's will, 'tis no wonder if there be heats and contests between you. Sin is the greatest makebate in the world: if you are not afraid of displeasing God, you will not be afraid of displeasing one another. *O then, if thou could'st so far govern thine own spirit as to take offense at nothing in thy Husband but what is sinful, thou would'st not be so angry with him as thou art. The Apostle saith*, Ephes. 4.26. Be angry, and sin not: or, *be angry with nothing, or for nothing, but what is sinful; for I find the learned Interpreters rendering the meaning thus*: Be not angry with the Person of one another, but his Sin, and be angry as much against that sin in thy self, as another. *Observe but this rule, and it will prevent abundance of contention that usually ariseth between such near Relations.*

10. If thou would'st prevent the raging of thine anger against thy Husband or thy Wife, take heed of the first beginnings of thy passion. We know when a fire is begun in an house, we do not stay quenching of it, till the house be all on flame; but if there be but a little fire kindled in any part of the house, if it be but a smoke, thou wilt say where is it, and thou art not quiet till thou hast found it out: so it should be when passions begin to rise, thy Soul begins to be on fire, and thou should'st be as much for quenching it at first rising, as thou would'st when thou seest fire break out in thine house at the very first. Perhaps a Dish of water may quench that now, that if thou stay'st till half an hour hence, it may take hold of such solid matter, as that it passeth all thy labor and industry to quench, and makes a pitiful ruin. So if thou observest thy choler from the beginning, seeing it begin to fume or kindle for some light or small offense, it is easy for thee to suppress it, and stay the course; but if it be once settled, and begin to swell, and thou stir it up, and inflame it, it will be hard for thee afterwards to quench it. A small spark, if nourished, will increase

to a furious flame; so there have been most fearful distempers of passion from very small beginnings, which have broken out into most fearful outrages. How often is it in a Family, that a little spark doth kindle a great fire. At first there may be but a word spoken amiss, that might easily have been passed over; but that word begets another, and another, and so grows to a most hideous flame. Sometimes it is between the nearest Relations, as Husband and Wife, that a contention doth arise between them for a very small matter, sometimes for the very gesture of the hand, or some spots on the apparel. Oh! a very slight ground for distaste, and it argues very little or no Grace in that heart that is displeased with such inconsiderable things with which God is not displeased at all. Sometimes it begins in the very countenance: the Wife thinks that her Husband looks not upon her with so pleasant a countenance as he was wont to do, and from thence she begins to have surmises and suspicions, and then comes to make misinterpretations, and from thence there comes a strangeness, and from being strange she begins to hearken to tales that are carried to her against her Husband, and to believe them, and to aggravate them: Then she begins to speak some hard words against him, and then to do him some ill offices, then break out into violent and eminent passions and actings against him, reviling him, casting false aspersions upon him, endeavoring to represent him to others as the vilest wretch living, laying such things to his charge as he is altogether innocent of, and then to deny all conjugal respects to him, and then wish she had never been related to him; and some go so far, as to use indirect means to extinguish the Relation. Others grow fond of other men, and so come to have unlawful intimacy with them: whereas had there been care taken by her at the beginning, all this might have been prevented, as the wise man saith, Prov. 17.14. *The beginning of strife is as one letteth out water;*

therefore leave off contention before it be meddled with: or before the breach be made so great as not to be repaired. So then when thy heart is first set on fire with anger, do thou presently endeavor to quench it with the water of the Spirit; for after thou art thoroughly inflamed, it will be too late to apply any remedy till the flame hath spent itself. But thou may'st say, *I fall into anger many times when I never meant it, and it hath overcome me before I am aware: how therefore should I prevent that which I did not fore-see, or free myself from it when it violently over-ruleth me?* To which I answer,

1. *If thou dost carefully watch over thy self, thou shalt easily perceive when thou art inclining to anger; for there are many signs which go before a storm, and many symptoms which discover Diseases before persons do fall into them:* So thou may'st easily discern in thy self many notes and signs of this furious and tempestuous storm, and raging fever of mind, unjust anger, before it break forth and show itself. Much pain, swelling of heart, discontent, and bitterness of spirit appear before it.

2. Anger doth not presently, as soon as entered into thy heart, over-rule thee, before (by increase of fuel) it be grown to a greater height than it had at first. The most furious anger attaineth not its full strength at first entrance, but by little and little increaseth like a flame, by taking hold of new matter; and the fire in the beginning thereof is easily suppressed: First, by not yielding obedience to an angry passion, nor believing her in anything that she saith or doth, to prompt thee to furious actions. Therefore if thou observest thy self like to be transported with choler, endeavor to retain thy self, and strive to moderate thy passions, and divert the infirmity that seeks to seize upon thee: give no ear to any incitements unto anger.

3. If thou would'st timely subdue thy anger, withdraw the food wherewith it is nourished. The most furious anger will soon

be mitigated, if it be not continually nourished with a new supply of matter: the fuel of anger is the multiplying of words. As nothing sooner than the wind causeth a small spark to burst out into a furious flame, so nothing sooner doth cause a small spark of anger to increase into a furious raging flame, than the wind of words. Do not then think to disgorge thy stomach of anger by vomiting out spleen in bitter words, for they only aggravate things for the continuing of anger. Do thou therefore use most modesty. Mildness of speech and lowness of voice doth so withdraw nourishment from the fire of anger, that it will soon of itself be extinguished.

4. If thine anger begin to arise, make some delay before thou speakest or dost anything. Give not place to wrath, let it not have vent by sudden or unadvised words. Anger smothered will languish, but let out will flame into further mischief. 'Tis some cure of passion to delay it; therefore Solomon saith, Prov. 19.11. The discretion of a man deferreth his anger, *and it is wisdom so to do; so 'tis thine honor, it's the glory of a man to pass by a transgression, not to take distaste at every offense. Therefore 'tis good to check thy precipitant motions by delay, and due recourse to reason, lest by following thy passion too close, thou run thy self into great inconveniencies. O by thy quickness and shortness of Spirit thou art transported into many indecencies, which dishonor God, and wound thy conscience: therefore do what thou canst to suppress thine anger as soon as it doth appear.* If this course were taken by Husbands and Wives, it would be an excellent means to prevent and suppress anger and discord between them.

11. If thou would'st not be angry with thy Husband or thy Wife, take heed of too much curiosity in observing every little thing or every trifle in thy Husband's or Wife's words or actions: If thou would'st not be angry, thou must past over a great many things and take no notice of them; thou must have a kind of holy

negligence of a great many things, and pass over, and see and not see, and turn away thine ears from many things; as in Eccles. 7.21. *Also take no heed unto all words that are spoken.* Many things that are spoken thou must let pass unregarded, many times hard sayings, or ill speeches, vain and undervaluing speeches, speeches spoken at random without occasion, without consideration, and without any real detriment to us, must not be taken notice of, to make them occasions of enmity and discord, or to break our own peace and tranquility. Thus Mr. Cotton on this wise. Therefore, I say, do not take notice of hard or slight speeches spoken against thy self, or vain impertinent words that do thee no personal prejudice. Paul took little notice of words spoken against him. 1 Cor. 3.4. *But with me it is a very small thing that I should be judged of you.* Never keep empty impertinent words in thy memory, for thy memory is not to be filled with trash, and all occasions of enmity and discord should be put out of thy mind; as in Levit. 19.18. When things done by thy Husband or Wife are not of any consequence, rather let him or her know that thou dost not take notice of them. But if thou wilt be taking notice of, or offended with everything that is done or spoken, it is impossible but there will be a great deal of disturbance between thy self and Husband.

    12. If thou hast an angry Husband or an angry Wife, and yet after all the means thou hast used to prevent his or her angry passions; yet if he or she remain froward and contentious upon every trifle, then observe this rule, That thou resolve to walk before thy Husband or thy Wife in a convincing way. Thy Wife is of a troublesome Spirit, and wrests every word that thou speakest, and gives thee railing and reviling speeches; thou canst not in any way meddle with her, but thou dost foul thy fingers: yet resolve with thy self that thou wilt not render her reviling for reviling; and though she be froward, yet thou wilt not deal frowardly with

her. Say within thy self, *I will do what I can to convince her in a constant way of Good, of Holiness, Justice and Righteousness; it may be I may melt her heart that way: I am resolved whatever evil she doth to me, I will do good to her.* Here is a peaceable Spirit indeed, and this is the way to keep peace between thy self and Wife. When means have been tried to quiet her Spirit, yet it cannot be done; yet walk convincingly before her, and a convincing conversation in a few months may prevail with her heart more than all the means that thou hast used. Take but this course, and thou wilt find in some time that the bitterness of her Spirit will be allayed. O then wait on the Lord, keep his way, walk strictly and inoffensively, and commit thy cause to God, and in time all the stirs and clamors of thy Wife will vanish away, and come to nothing, and she will be at last convinced, and say that thou art a faithful Servant of God.

13. If thou would'st live in peace with thy Husband or thy Wife, be much in secret prayer, earnestly importuning God that he would mortify thy angry passions. Prayer is an excellent spiritual help to prevent frowardness and discord between Husband and Wife. Thou may'st cry out of the contentions that are between thy self and Husband, of the bitterness of his Spirit, and that he is an offense to thee: but I appeal this day in the name of God to thy conscience, what time hast thou spent in secret prayer to make thy moan to God, to complain to God in secret between God and thy Soul? Perhaps when thou art in more public Prayer, thou may'st pray God to heal the breaches between thee and thy Husband, or thy Wife: but when thou hast been in secret, hast thou poured out thy heart with earnest prayer, that God would find out means of reconciliation. Say unto the Lord. *There is a great distance between myself and Wife, or between myself and Husband, and I find all means that I use ineffectual to make up the*

breaches between us: But, Lord, thou knowest how to still the rage of my Wife's spirit, thou knowest how to compose differences between us. Do it, Lord, I humbly pray thee. Oh I pray thee, O gracious God, to vouchsafe the assistance of thy Spirit to subdue mine anger, or my Wife's anger, that both our affections may be so ruled and sanctified, that they being freed from natural corruption, may be made fit and serviceable for the setting forth of thy glory, and the mutual good, peace and comfort of each other, and the furthering one another's Salvation. This is the most excellent means to prevent frowardness and contention between Husband and Wife; for it is only the water of the Spirit, and the Shield of Faith, which is able to quench the fury of our passions, of which Prayer is the chief means of obtaining, and then we shall find that what cannot be done at all by our strength and skill, may be easily done by God's assistance and direction.

Thus, O Husband, and O Wife, I have given several directions how you may prevent anger and discord between each other: And O that the Lord would give you hearts to follow them. And therefore let me give you some arguments to press you to use those helps and directions for the restraining and suppressing your angry passions; and that very briefly.

1. Thou should'st take care to use means to suppress and prevent thy angry passions, because the furiousness and disquiet of a person's spirit hinders that person from Communion with God; it keeps him or her from intimacy with, and comfortable enjoyments of God. As God forbids men, Prov. 22.24. *to make any friendship with an angry person, neither to go with a furious man, lest they learn his ways, and receive destruction to their Souls.* That is, avoid the company of those who are angry and choleric, lest by a certain contagion they poison thee with their passions. Indeed so will God withdraw from such as he commands us to

withdraw from, and should'st thou not watch against evil, that will make thee to be without God in the world? 'Tis sad indeed to do anything to cause the withdrawments of God; for as soon as God departs from a Soul, the Devil visits it: therefore it is said, *That a giving way to wrath, is a giving place to the Devil*. Oh what a miserable exchange is this! and what a sad loss is it to lose God! and when God is driven away by the excess of angry passions, there is a loss of that sweet and holy disposition of Soul which ought to be in every Christian, and is in every one that walketh in peace and fellowship with God, in true peace of conscience. As there is required reconciliation with God, and a sense of his love, so likewise a freedom from the hurry of boisterous passions, and a calmness of spirit, which is a necessary qualification in the subject capable to hold Communion with God, and receive the beams of his favor. O consider this seriously, Dost thou think it nothing to be without the blessing of God? Alas! then thou losest God's protection and guidance in times of danger, who then shall help thee in thy straights, or direct thee in times of darkness and doubtings, when the Original of all Power and the Fountain of all Wisdom hath left thee? Indeed if thou let thy angry passions to rage upon every trifling occasion, thou dost not only provoke God to be gone from thee, but to be gone in distaste. 'Tis sad when God conceals himself but a little while from a poor Soul, and clouds his presence a little while. A gracious Soul cannot bear a little withholding of God from it, when he lets out no intimations of displeasure: but how terrible are the withdrawments of God, when he withdraws in high displeasure, and thou knowest not whether he will ever return again in mercy, or not? And it is said in 2 Sam. 22.27. *And with the froward thou wilt shew thy self unsavory*. The Hebrew hath it, *With the perverse thou behavest thy self as one turned about*; and that the very thoughts of God will be unsavory and unpleasant thoughts to them. Angry froward persons shall not have the least discovery or sense of God's love while they are in their fits, nor much at other times, because *an angry froward frame of spirit is an abomination to the Lord*, Prov. 3.32. and chap. 8.13. and 11.20. As frowardness causeth strife between the nearest Relations, so it makes contention between God and the Soul. The angry froward person opposeth God, and God opposeth that person: So that hence it appears that thou hast abundant cause and reason to use all possible means to restrain and suppress thy angry passions, because they hinder thee from enjoying the divine Presence, and the blessed discoveries of divine Favor.

2. Thou should'st take great care to restrain and suppress thy angry passions, and hasty frowardness of spirit, because as they prevail, thy actings are as contrary to true grace, as anything almost that thou canst think of, and truly there may be a great deal of suspicion whether thou hast true Grace, or no. I conceive there may be some Analogy between a Nazarite and a gracious Soul. It is said in Numb. 6.2. *That the Nazarites were to separate themselves unto the Lord.* They were to be separated from the ordinary course of that they might more freely and wholly dedicate themselves to the service of God, and to a more strict and pure course of serving God, than other men used; and indeed God confined them to strict rules: They were to abstain from anything that did belong to the Vine; hereby also signifying a full and perfect renouncing all worldly pleasures, or anything tending thereunto; intimating, that they were not only to *abstain from all evil, but all appearances of evil*, 1 Thes. 5.22. All the outward Ceremonies enjoined them, were but Types of inward Holiness. I take notice of one thing enjoined them, which is most especially to my purpose, which is, That they should drink no Vinegar of Wine, or

any other strong Liquor; that was to signify, that they must not be of Vinegar Spirits, of sour and eager Spirits, but of quiet Spirits, of loving and meek Spirits. Now all the Saints of God they are Nazarites. As Christ was a Nazarite, so all that are Christ's are Nazarites seperated from others to be the Lord's people. The Lord separates the godly man for himself, as in Psal. 4.3 *But know that the Lord hath set apart him that is godly for himself*; and they must not be of harsh and hot Spirits, but should be adorned with this lovely amiable grace of meekness: so that a hasty, froward and passionate Spirit is directly opposite to a meek, patient, and quiet Spirit; and if there be any grace in a furious person, it is raked up under a great deal of ashes of corruption, that it is not easily discerned. Now the opposition that anger and frowardness bears to Grace appears,

    1. If thou dost consider what it is that Grace doth in the heart when it first comes, the first thing is to show unto the Soul its own vileness, its own wretchedness and baseness by sin, and the danger that it is in through sin. Now a froward passionate heart is very contrary to the sight of its own baseness and vileness; for thou canst not see thy self to be a base, vile, sinful worm, and yet bear nothing that is against thee, but presently thy heart is in a flame if anything doth cross thee; for thou could'st not be so angry, if thou didst not think thy self too great and too good to be crossed.

    2. When Grace comes into the heart, it brings the heart into subjection unto God, and unto another rule than it walked by before. That's a principal work of Grace, to subdue the heart of a sinner unto God. The hearts of sinners are naturally stout, and rebellious against God, and goes on in a stubborn way, till Grace comes, and lays them under; but a froward and passionate heart would be indeed above God, and any of his rules. It cannot

keep itself under, and lie in subjection unto rule; and hence is the reason that froward and passionate people used to have such expressions, *I will, nay but I will*, and *I care not*, their hearts are subdued to the authority of God. But the heart that is subdued to the Lord, bring it but a Scripture, and it yields presently; but a froward Spirit is not so. How contrary then is frowardness to Grace? I might instance in many other particulars, but I shall be too large then. O then, is passion and frowardness so opposite to Grace? doth it either hinder the working of grace in the heart, or at least weaken, yea, smother grace, that it is almost extinguished, though not totally, yet so as it is not easily discernable? Dost thou not then see great reason to use all means to mortify thy passions.

3. Thou should'st use thy utmost endeavors to mortify thy passions, and live in peace with thy Husband or thy Wife, because thou dost manifest a truly noble and generous Spirit, if thou would'st pass by offenses without manifesting anger and frowardness of Spirit. To this effect speaks Solomon, Prov. 19.11. *It is the Glory of a man to pass by a transgression*; that is, not to manifest an angry displeasure for an offense that another doth him. And so we say when we restrain our anger against another for anything done amiss, *I will pass you by for this time, I will not take any severe notice of what you have done.* O it is an honorable thing to bridle anger when a person is offended, to wink at smaller infirmities, and remit greater wrongs. Generous Spirits are (as it were) impenetrable by offenses; yea, a Spirit truly elevated, a generous and noble Soul, is always quiet, moderate, and grave, never suffering itself to be transported with the violent motions of choler. Certainly a meek person hath a magnanimous and heroic Spirit. See what the wise man saith in Prov. 16.32. *He that is slow to anger, is better than the mighty; and he that ruleth his Spirit, than he that taketh a City*. He that overcometh himself, is stronger than

one that overcometh a City. Now it is a glorious thing for a Soldier to overcome a City, but one that can overcome his own passion, is more valiant, and hath a more excellent Spirit, than one that overcomes a great City. And so some Creatures that are more heroic, are more meek and gentle than others are; The Lion is of a more generous Spirit than the Wolf is. The more honorable any one is, the more he is of a peaceable disposition, and his anger is sooner pacified. It is enough to fall down before a Lion, a Lion is pacified if you fall before him: but not the Wolf and Tiger, and other baser Creatures, they will tear those that fall down before them. Hence observe, such as are soon moved to violent passions, that will not pass by a slight offense, but will be furious for every trifle, they are of ignoble, base, sordid tempers, of vile, wretched, and dunghill dispositions. O then, what care should'st thou take to watch against the first risings of anger, and faithfully endeavor to suppress thy violent passions when risen, to wink and connive at many offenses! If ever thou wilt evidence a noble Spirit, it is thy true glory so to do; but 'tis thy ignominy and disgrace to be of a Gunpowder-Spirit, to be transported into a flame of fury by every little spark of distaste given. Nay, a furious Spirit is a devilish Spirit, and therefore the Devils are very often called Furies. O let this consideration stir thee up to endeavor after meekness, calmness, and peaceableness of Spirit.

4. Thou should'st be careful to abstain from anger and frowardness of Spirit, because there is nothing that thou canst do in anger, but thou may'st do it better out of anger. Thou canst have thy mind or thy will in nothing in anger, but thou may'st have thy mind and will better out of an angry fit. And wherefore then should'st thou be angry? Consider when thou hast thine anger stirring, what thou would'st do in thine anger. Thou may it say, *I would reprove my Wife or my Husband that hath done amiss.* I say,

thou must reprove without anger, thou must *restore with a spirit of meekness*, Gal. 6.1. There is no recovering a fallen Relation from sin in a boisterous way. There are gentle means, that are most influential. Thy reproof should be as Physic: thou dost not used to give Physic scalding hot. Thou may'st reprove thy Wife, Husband, Child, or Servant, without anger, as well as with anger; and if thou would'st give correction, thou may'st do it best without anger. If thou dost correct in anger, or reprove in anger, thy Servant or any other Relation will think it is rather from *thy fury* than *his fault* that thou do'st it. Perhaps thou would'st do some special service for God, and thou say'st that anger will quicken thee: But James saith, cap. 1.20. *The wrath of man accomplisheth not the righteousness of God*. God will not be beholding to the wrath of man for anything. An Heathen could say, *That Fortitude had no need of wrath, no need of gall, bitterness and choler, but it may be well enough without it*. Perhaps thou would'st make thine Husband sensible of the wrong he had done thee: That thou may'st do without anger. If he hath wronged thee, show him the more respect and kindness; this way thou shalt make him sensible of the wrong he hath done thee, as well as any way in the world, that it will either melt his heart, or trouble his Spirit, till he hath made thee restitution, or confessed his fault. I say, everything can be better done in a calm and quiet frame, than in an angry fit; for in thine anger thou canst not so well exercise thy reason as at another time; for the fire of passion, when it is kindled, causeth a great smoke to come up to the Understanding and Judgment, and even puts out thy Reason. So that is very great reason why thou should'st use all means to prevent and suppress thine angry passions.

    5. Thou should'st do thy utmost to refrain from anger, and attain meekness of spirit, because meekness is that grace whereby men and women come to have fair weather all the year

long. It is a comfortable thing to have fair weather to continue but two or three weeks together, and thou knowest that rainy weather and dropping weather is very tedious and irksome to us, and we say, *It is pity fair weather should do any hurt*: But when Husband and Wife are both meek, there is fair weather in that Family every day, all the week long. But where they are froward and passionate, there is rainy weather all the week long. Solomon sets out passion and frowardness by *a continual dropping*, Prov. 19.13. *And the contentions of a Wife are a continual dropping*; her scolding and brawling may occasion much sadness, trouble, and hurt in the Family. And so in Prov. 27.15. *A continual dropping in a very rainy day, and a contentious woman, are alike.* The Hebrew renders it, A continual dropping in a day of a great shower of rain, and a Wife of brawlings and contentions, are alike. Where the rain drops into an house, it is very troublesome; but when the Sun comes in at the window, there is a sweet and pleasant dwelling, that is comfortable. Many times thou knowest that the Sun riseth very fair in the morning, but it rains mightily before night: So in many Families, though there is a great deal of quietness in the morning, and there seemeth to be a great deal of love between Husband and Wife, yet what a storm is there before night! and the reason is, because a passionate person looks on that as a great crime, which a meek person can see no evil at all in. Where there is meekness, there fair weather continues always. Now, though passion and frowardness be uncomely amongst all, and meekness is lovely in all. But passion is more uncomely, and meekness is more sweet and lovely between Man and Wife: they should walk sweetly and lovingly together when God by such an Ordinance of his hath so united them in such a way of Communion as they are united. Such God hath joined by the holy Ordinance of Marriage, that indeed is a greater bond than the bond of Nature; *for a man and woman must forsake all Relations, and cleave to one another, and of twain become one flesh.* And should they not be of one mind? O then, how careful should Husband and Wife be to avoid those angry passions that hinder that sweetness, comfort, and delight which they might enjoy, were they of patient and meek Spirits! Meekness of Spirit makes them very careful in discharging mutual duties to each other, and that keeps fair weather between them: but passion makes them oppose the commands of the Gospel, and that makes tempestuous weather between them. The Scripture says, *Wives, see that you reverence your Husbands*: when then thou dost provoke thy Husband, and speak it to him in a froward way, I appeal to thy conscience, *Dost thou reverence thy Husband?* Thou may'st say, *he doth not deserve it.* Whether he deserve it or no, thou art to reverence him; thou must reverence him in words, gestures, actions, and in thy very heart, and not give him insolent and reflecting language, or like Zipporah, Exod. 4.25, 26. call him *a bloody Husband.* God hath made Marriage a union for communion, for love, for help, for peace, for delight; and thou dost by thy angry passions do what in thee lies to frustrate the very Ordinance of God. Know, that God will not bear it at thine hands, to frustrate that great Ordinance of his. Let the Wife then consider the Husband as one that God commands *that she should reverence and obey in all things that are not sinful*; and let the Husband consider the Wife as the weaker Vessel, and bear with her sinless infirmities: This is the way to keep fair and comfortable weather always between them. But the Wife may come under the first head of Inferiors. God hath put her in an inferior condition, and therefore frowardness and passion is very uncomely in her. O then, as ever you would prevent tempestuous weather between you, as ever you would maintain love, comfort, and quietness between you, strive to refrain from angry passions, endeavor to get yourselves adorned with the grace of meekness. Remember still you are one flesh, and therefore be no more offended with the words and failings of each other, than you would if they were your own, for you cannot be free from failings till you have attained full perfection, which is not to be gotten in this life. Fall out no more with your Husbands or with your Wives for their words or faulty actions, than you would with yourselves for your own faults, or your own words of common and ordinary discourse. This will allow you such an anger or displeasure against a fault, as tendeth to heal it, but not such as tendeth to vex and fester the diseased part. This will turn anger into compassion, and a speedy diligence for the cure. Consider this, I pray, and avoid all occasions of wrath and falling out: Do not do anything to contract a discontented peevish habit; do not in your impatience wrangle and disquiet one another, speak not reproachful and provoking words, talking hotly doth blow the fire, and increase the flame. Be but silent, and you will sooner return to your serenity and peace. Some calm and condescending words of reason may stop the torrent, and revive the reason which passion had overcome. Foul words, as they tend to disgrace and displease one another, so they produce many evil effects. After Thunder comes Rain. Do not then cast on Oil or Fuel, by answering one another provokingly or sharply, or by multiplying words, or by answering wrath with wrath. You must endeavor to mollify, and not exasperate one another. O that arguments might prevail with you to take this course! O then in how much sweetness, amity, and peace might you live with one another!

6. Consider that no excuse or pretense whatsoever can justify your being angry with one another. Thou may'st say perhaps, *O Husband, or O wife, I am of a very hasty and choleric nature, and cannot leave it, but shall be soon angry when occasion is*

given. This vain excuse is no better than Adam's fig-leaves to hide the nakedness of sin, and will not justify thy furious passions; for if thou art of a passionate nature, thou hast a nature that is abominable to God. Prov. 3.32. *For the froward is an abomination to the Lord*; that is, which God esteemeth and accounteth an abomination; for when the heart is froward, *the person deviseth mischief continually; and soweth discord*, cap. 6.14. This frowardness in the heart, as it intimates perverseness of the heart, so also a passionate nature: So none are more obstinate and perverse than angry persons, and are the causers of great dissentions and disagreements; and therefore such God hates, because *he loveth transgression that loveth strife*, cap. 17.19. An angry nature is always brawling, and contention is the original cause of many sins, which the contentious person by his actings seemeth to love: therefore do not plead thy nature by way of excuse. If thy nature be choleric, it is not the nature that God created thee in, for God made man upright, *after his own Image*, like himself, who is *slow to anger*. It is the glory of God to be slow to wrath, and thy froward nature is not God's nature, it is but thy original corruption. Thou art froward, and thy original corruption is in the strength of it. Is this any lessening of the evil of the root, because it hath corrupt branches? or will it lessen the evil of a Child, because it had a wicked Father? And therefore thou art not to excuse one sin with another, but rather earnestly labor that this pollution may be washed away with the water of God's Spirit, who by his *Grace* doth reform *Nature*. If thou art of such a wicked disposition that thou canst not but be angry, thy sin is the more heinous, and thy state the more dangerous; for *rooted sickness* is worse than *new-bred*, an *old sore* than a *green wound*. The sins that are set most deep in nature, are most hateful and dangerous: therefore thy being of a choleric nature should be thy *humiliation*, not thy *excuse*; for if thou hast nothing but nature, nothing to overcome thy nature, thou shalt never go to Heaven; for every man and woman in the world, that hath the least degree of grace, is made partaker of the Divine Nature, Now the Divine Nature, that prevails, reigns, and rules in the heart; therefore to plead *Nature* to excuse *Anger*, is as much as to say, *I am yet the child of wrath, therefore I cannot cease to be angry.* O thou may'st say, *I am flesh and blood, and how can I be able to be of such a quiet and meek spirit when I am wronged?* indeed it is very difficult. 'Tis true, all good things are difficult, and meekness would not be so excellent a grace, were it not difficult to attain: but it is difficult only to those that have no gracious principles in them. An endeavor to conquer thy passions may seem difficult at first; but try once or twice, and thou wilt find so much sweetness in thy spirit, that it will not appear so difficult, but find *this yoke of Christ very easy*: and though thou art flesh and blood, yet thou hast Reason to rule flesh and blood. If thou art but flesh and blood, shall vile flesh and blood take so much upon it, as (if it be crossed in anything) to fly in the face of God, and revile thy dearest Relation, and cross God's will. 'Tis sad that flesh and blood should do this. And I tell thee, if ever thou be saved, thou must be more than flesh and blood, for flesh and blood shall never enter into the Kingdom of Heaven. But thou may'st say, *I am greatly provoked, I should live quietly with my Husband, and in my Family, except I be provoked; and it is his fault who provokes me, rather than mine who am angry.* I answer, *There was no need indeed of the grace of meekness, if there was nothing to provoke thee. The Devil is meek when he's pleased: but for thee to say that thou art meek, whereas thou art meek only when thou art pleased, that is no meekness. Now is the time for thee to exercise meekness when thou art provoked, to forbear angry passions when thou art crossed. To say thou art froward only when thou art provoked, is as much as to say*, I am not froward, but when God calls upon me to exercise meekness: *For whenever thou art provoked, that is the proper time to exercise meekness. And it is a sign of a very carnal heart, to put off thy sin to the temptation; that when thou hast done evil, thou say'st,* Such an one did provoke me to it, or this wicked Devil did tempt me to it: *whereas it were only thy corruptions that made thee furious; whereas those that are truly gracious, and are of tender spirits, are ready to charge themselves to the uttermost for any evil. They judge that all the evil of their lives doth arise from the wicked corruptions of their hearts: but a carnal heart will charge temptation with all, and would free himself, and discharge his corruptions from that which doth arise wholly from corruption, and from no other principle. So that it is more of inward corruption than outward provocation that thou art so passionate. A little occasion may provoke thee to passion, but a great matter will not provoke thee to good works. Why should anything provoke thee do thy self a mischief? Thou canst not provoke a Beast (with all the blows thou canst give him) to leap into the fire: and why art thou so easily provoked to mischief thy self in the fire of passion?* O consider how thou dost provoke God continually, and thou should'st labor to be as God is. He is not so angry upon all thy provocations as to fly upon thee: He can bear, though thou provoke him, and why should'st thou not bear when thy fellow-Creatures provoke thee? Perhaps thou may'st say, *There was never any one so abused as I am; never any one had such an Husband as I have. I answer, Certainly this is the pride of thy heart to think or say so. A proud heart being great itself, makes every little affliction, every little cross seem great. By reason of thy pride of heart thou thinkest it a great matter to suffer any little thing. Hadst thou an humble heart, thou would'st not think it a great matter to suffer, and know that God is more abused every day, than thou art, or ever could'st be. An humble heart says,* Doth the

Lord send such afflictions upon me more than on any other? The Lord sees I have a more vile heart than any other, and therefore I deserve more afflictions than another. *And certainly if thou art more froward than others, therefore thou dost meet with more evil than others, because thou art a froward person. The Lord sees thy heart so vile in thy frowardness, that thou tenderest not God's glory, therefore he tenders not thy good. There is no person in the world that doth meet with so much occasion of vexation, as a froward person doth: and if thou didst but pass a right judgment, thou would'st find that others suffer as much as thou dost, nay more, yea, it may be they suffer more by thee than thou dost by them: thou art more an afflicter to them, than they are to thee. So that it is clear that no pretense or excuse that thou canst make can justify thy angry passions with thy Husband or with thy Wife, but still thy passions will be sinful. And should'st thou not then do thy utmost to restrain and suppress thy violent passions? should not such a consideration make thee cease contending with so near a Relation as an Husband or a Wife? Pray then mind the directions given thee to prevent thy furiousness of spirit.*

7. Thou should'st be very watchful against thy anger and frowardness of spirit, because nothing in the world doth more discover thy shame and folly, than thy angry passion. Therefore 'tis observable how many times the Scripture couples anger and folly together, and makes passionate people the foolishest people in the world. When thou art provoked, thy passion doth discover what is in thee, which is not discovered until then. Whatever shameful thing is in thee, will quickly discover itself in thine anger. Indeed thy carriage is so foul and vile in thy passion, that thy nearest Relation is ashamed of thee. Certainly one would wonder to see the shameful carriage of some men and women in their passions. I have heard of a Wife that fell out with her Husband

for a trifle, only for the moving of his hand in ordinary discourse; and because by her bitter provoking speeches she could not move him to the like furiousness of spirit, she told him, H*e was of a gangrene spirit, and that he was of so sordid and base dunghill spirit, that nothing would move him*; and fretted the more exceedingly, that he did bear her railings so patiently: For he knowing that the Scripture forbad him to render reviling for reviling, bore all her provocations with admirable patience. Also I have heard of a Wife, when her Husband would not do such things as she would have him, (which he did judge not convenient to be done) she would pluck him by the hair, sometimes strike him on the face, sometimes on the head. At divers other times in her rage (which she would be often in, she knew not why herself,) she would give him such insulting, bitter, reviling, reproachful, disdainful, and imperious speeches, as are not fit to be mentioned. Both these persons I knew myself, and do know what I have written to be true; and I have mentioned this instance to show the shameful acts that persons are guilty of in their passions. Some Wives are so proud and passionate, that nothing but a submissive obedience to their insolent and unreasonable commands will gratify them; and if their Husbands think it too much to be subject to the commands of an inferior, they shall not be permitted to live in quiet. And I know one Wife that told her Husband, for not gratifying her perverse humor, *that it was no matter if he had been buried alive, rather than have married her*. And also I have known an Husband who in his furious passion said, *that he did wish the Devil would come and fetch away his Wife*, who was a serious, holy, and meek woman. And should'st thou not be ashamed of thy passions, that make thee guilty of such shameful carriages? Indeed in such shameful carriages passionate people discover the greatest folly imaginable. O then it is great folly to give way to anger, therefore Solomon in

Eccles. 7.9. saith, *that anger resteth in the bosom of fools*; and in Prov. 12.16. *A fools wrath is presently known, but a prudent man covereth his shame.* A fools wrath is known by his words, actions, and gestures; his wrath is vented in rash and ill-advised speeches, which hurt his Neighbor, whereby the folly of the angry person is discovered, and so discovers his or her shame. But a prudent man (that is, a meek man) by his forbearing to be angry covereth his shame. And in Prov. 14.17. it is said, *He that is soon angry dealeth foolishly*: and in ver. 29. *He that is slow to wrath, is of great understanding: but he that is hasty of spirit, exalteth folly.* The meek person hath much understanding, which he discovereth by this, in that he knoweth how to bear wrongs and injuries patiently, and can beware of doing anything that doth truly oppose Honor and Virtue: But he or she that is hasty of mind, or short of spirit, that is soon angry, *exalteth folly*; that is, bringeth his folly to open light, to be seen of all men, forasmuch as he or she doth in his or her anger those things which cannot consist with Honor and Virtue. Thus continually the Scripture doth befool passionate people, and it is to check froward people, because there are none that think themselves wiser than angry people do, especially in the time of their fit. Certainly, because angry persons discover great folly in opening their shame, they make evident what filthy trash was closeted up in their hearts, which was not known before. Alas! of what ridiculous, rude, and indiscreet actions are angry persons daily guilty of; they will reverence no Superior, respect no Equal, but contemn all that oppose their humor. Their chief work is railing and vilifying others much superior to themselves in real worth: They are exceeding talkative, all others must hold their peace but themselves: and in the multitude of their words there wanteth not folly. But in all these insolent, imperious, and insulting carriages of a Wife to her Husband, where is the reverence and observance that God requires her to give him? for reverence is due to a man as he is an Husband; to the bad Husband, as well as to the good; to the poor Husband, as well as to the rich: So that no defect of the Husband can excuse the Wife from giving him due reverence and subjection to his superiority. So that all the irreverent speeches she gives her Husband in her passion, are but the discoveries of her shame and folly.

    I have now ended my Arguments and Motives which I have laid before you to persuade you to use the directions that I have here given to prevent Wrath and Discord between Husband and Wife. Pray then let those considerations influence you to watch against your angry passions; do not allow yourselves in that which discovers so much of your shame and folly, that such near Relations by their furious carriages one to another should make themselves ridiculous to all that know them, is very sad. You are one flesh, be of one spirit and one heart, be faithful to discharge the duty you owe to one another. Be not too curious in observing every look or gesture of one another. Wink at everything that crosseth you, so long as it doth not cross the will of God. Let each of you keep in your own station. Let not the Wife look for superiority, when God hath appointed her subjection. Let her not be ambitious of teaching, when her place is to be a learner. A cheerful subjection to God's Ordinances, and a ready delightful submission to God's providential appointments, is an excellent means to keep peace, and prevent contentions between Man and Wife. It is a great occasion of strife, when that party will prescribe rules to the other, that ought to be ruled by the other. Do not discover your folly by your insolent carriages one to another. Do not allow your passions, that will make you utter such expressions that will prove your shame. Be willing to live in peace one with another. And therefore be persuaded by the Arguments and Motives that I have here given, to use the direction now laid before you, to prevent Wrath and Discord between you.

Soli Deo Gloria

FINIS

THE APPENDIX

Some Wives plead in excuse of their froward carriages to their Husbands thus: *None ought to account my zeal for God's glory in a smart reprehension of my Husband's miscarriages, to be sinful anger; for I must not let my Husband alone to dishonor God, because my not appearing for God when my Husband offends him, will intimate an approbation of his sinful ways. I cannot be faithful to God, except I do oppose him in such actions as I conceive are not good: and in this respect I judge not myself blameworthy in contending with him. Is it not my duty to reprove my Husband when he offends God, and deals injuriously with me?*

Meeting with this Plea since I composed the foregoing *Treatise*, I have added this following *Answer*, as an *Appendix* to the former discourse; which is, *That I do acknowledge that some endeavors may be used by Wives to convince their Husbands of their sins, and to reform their conversations.* But by an explanation of the nature of *Reproof* it will appear what method is proper to be used by Wives to reclaim their Husbands from their disorderly walkings. To *Reprove* in a strict sense denotes an authority in the *Reprover* over the *Reproved*; for reproving is an act of authority, which a person hath by virtue of *Office* or *Relation*; as in Tit. 2.15. *Rebuke with all authority*: In this sense a superior is not to be reproved. Therefore the Apostle saith, 1 Tim. 5.1. *Rebuke not an Elder*. I understand it not only of the *Aged*, but of all *Superiors* in Place and Dignity; a tart reprehension, or a direct reproof, is not to be given them by Inferiors: they are to be dealt with as Fathers are to be dealt with by their Children, they may be *desired*, but not *rebuked*. Entreat them as a Father. *Admonitions* are given by such as are Equals of the same Degree and Quality, of the same Ecclesiastical Corporation, or Christian Society, which are either finding fault with each other for sins committed, or persuading or exhorting unto duties which have been omitted: And I look on admonitions to be of a more inferior quality than the rebukes which Superiors give to their Inferiors; for although an admonition be given as an act of Duty, yet not as an act of Authority, as the other is. But that way which I conceive an Inferior may take to reclaim a Superior from sin, and yet not go out of his place, or usurp authority which belongs not to him, is by an humble, earnest, and respectful entreating the Superior to forbear his sinful acts, which God hath prohibited him to concern himself with, and to engage in those Christian duties which God requires him to perform. So that I acknowledge that there is a time when in a limited sense inferiors may use means to hinder their Superiors going on in a way of sin. Job. 31.13. Superiors are not above instruction or humble advice, their authority doth not give them a toleration to persevere in sin, nor a liberty to trample their inferiors under their feet. Though we are under our Superior's Power, yet we are not under their Lusts; though we are to be governed by them, yet not to be despised by them. As we ought to serve, so they ought to govern, in the fear of God; and Superior's irregularities are to be hinted to them in an humble manner, and Superiors ought to act as men accountable to an Higher Power; and those which are above others on Earth, are to be informed when they offend God in Heaven. He which is

Superior in one respect, is *Inferior* in another. The Husband which hath Dominion over his Wife, is under God's Dominion. Though he is above his Wife, yet he is not above God's Law. God's Law must oblige the Husband as well as the Wife; and when the Husband breaks God's Law, he may be lawfully told of it by his Wife in a regular and humble manner, so that she doth always manifest a reverence to the superiority God hath placed in her Husband.

But many Wives think that they are not at all inferior to their Husbands. They conclude that they are equal with them in all things, because by the Marriage-relation they become one flesh. Other Wives are not satisfied, except their Husbands carry it towards them as persons subordinate to them, and in the pride of their spirits speak to their Husbands in such masterly language as to their Inferiors, and will revile their Husbands if they do not in everything subject themselves to their cross, perverse, and froward humors, and bear with all their insolent carriages; and this they will do under pretense of reproving their Husbands miscarriages; and they will be always contending with their Husbands, if their Husbands will not submit to be in subjection to them, whereby they seldom live in peace with each other.

In order to the reformation of this great disorder in Wives carriages to their Husbands;

1. I shall endeavor to convince them that their Husbands have a right of superiority over them.

2. I shall give some cautions to Wives to prevent their insulting over their Husbands under a pretense of reproving their faults, that they may not presume to exercise any kind of authority over them, that God requires them to be subject unto, and therein acquaint them with the proper method God allows them to take in admonishing their Husbands.

3. I shall direct them both how to carry themselves to

those that are subordinate to them both; for their proper carriage to their inferiors in their Families will be a special help to preserve peace between them.

1. *To prove the Husband's right of superiority over the Wife.*

1. Consider, that the titles given the Husband in Scripture doth prove his superiority and the Wife's subjection. The Husband is called *the Wife's Lord*, 1 Pet. 3.5, 6. *Being in subjection to their own Husbands, even as Sarah obeyed Abraham, calling him Lord.* So in Gen. 18.12. He is her *Master*, Est. 1.17, 22. *Her Head*, 1 Cor. 11.3. *Her Guide*, Prov. 2.17. *She forsaketh the guide of her youth*; which is meant of her Husband, whom she married in her youth, and whom by marriage she received as the guide of her youth under God, who is to be her guide both in youth and old age, and by forsaking the government of her Husband in his commands, directions and counsels, she forgetteth the Covenant of God made in marriage. All these expressions do evince the Husband's superiority and the Wive's subordination and orderly subjection.

2. The Wife was made after man, therefore she should not go before man. 1 Tim. 2.12, 13. Adam *was first formed, then Eve*; therefore she must not usurp authority over the man; she must not be a Teacher, but a Learner in silence with all subjection; Teaching and reproving is taking an authority upon her which belongs not to her. The *Woman was made of Man*, 1 Cor. 11.8. she received her being (under God) from man: now the Effect is ever less noble, and inferior to the Cause. The woman was made for man, 1 Cor. 11.9. that which serveth to any end, is less than the end to which it serveth. And *the woman is the glory of the man*, 1 Cor. 11.7. as he hath so excellent a Creature as a Woman endued with reason, as himself, subject to him. Dominion in this case being man's privilege, Gen. 3.16. *Thy desire shall be to thy Husband,*

and he shall rule over thee. The superiority that God hath given man to enjoy, shall he not enjoy it as God hath given it. Ephes. 5.22, 23, 24. *Wives submit yourselves unto your own Husbands, as to the Lord*. Some Wives are not convinced that they owe this subjection to their Husbands as the Scripture requireth, but in truth every Wife owes it to her own Husband, Though he comes short of others in Knowledge, Wisdom, Education, Estate, and every other thing which doth deserve it. For the great and main duty which a Wife (as a Wife) ought to learn, and so learn as to practice, is, to be subject to her Husband; and Paul holds it forth as the sum of all other duties. And there is no Wife, whatever be her Birth, Parts, Portion, Breeding, or any other Privilege, who is exempted from this tie of *subjection to her own Husband*: The Law of Nature, God's Ordinance, and her own voluntary Covenant, binds her to it; and there is not any Husband to whom this honor of *subjection* is not due; no personal infirmities, frowardness of nature, no nor error in point of Religion, doth deprive him of it, provided her submission be in those things which are consistent with her love to Christ. And the Wife's subjection ought to flow from the conscience of, and respect to that state and dignity wherein God hath placed her Husband above her, which ought to engage her to reverence, and obey him. For, as I said before, *the Husband is the Head of the Wife*, and this *subjection to the Husband ought to be in every thing* (Ephes. 5.24.) which is not forbidden in the word of God, Though it cross the humor of the Wife, and argue little discretion in the Husband that commandeth it.

    3. Wives are obliged to be in subjection to their Husbands by their Marriage-Covenants, wherein they have promised *Obedience to their Husbands*: and Marriage-promises must be performed. Now, *Obedience* is an act of subjection, and an evidence of inferiority: so that such Wives as are not willing to consent

to their Husbands superiority, are not willing to be faithful to their own engagements. Indeed God will be very severe against such women as make no conscience of observing their Marriage-covenant, for it is God's Covenant made in his name. God is the Author of it, as he is the Ordainer of that state of Marriage: and it is made in God's presence, so he is a witness to it. Mal. 2.14. *And this Covenant is God's Covenant, because he will avenge the breach of it.* God will certainly severely avenge the quarrel of his Covenant, when men and women are the only expressed parties in the Covenant; and God made Zedekiah smart sorely for breaking his Covenant with the King of Babylon. Ezek. 17.16, 19. Zedekiah *gave his band to confirm his Covenant made to the King of Babylon, that he would be subject to him*: so Wives give their hands to their Husbands in Marriage, *that they will be obedient to them*: They cannot look upon their own hands, and not remember how they were engaged. So that God swears, *As sure as I am God, you shall feel the weight of my displeasure for your perfidiousness.* The King of Heaven doth regard his Oath, and if the Lord once swear, he will perform, and there shall be no escaping of what he hath threatened. Indeed, as I said before, Oaths and Covenants made with men are Divine things, and not to be slighted. The Covenant that was made with an Heathenish King, and an Idolater, God owns as made with himself, because his sacred and dreadful Name was used therein: therefore God said, Mine Oath that he hath despised, and Covenant that he hath broken. Violating of Covenants falsifying of promises, and perfidious doings, are exceeding evil, and God will make such as violate their own word exemplary to all the world, and they shall live in perpetual infamy. So if Wives forget the Covenant of their God made in Marriage, God will remember their forgetfulness, and recompense their Perjury upon their own heads; for every disobedient

Wife is in a sense a perjured Wife, and if they think to loose the bonds of this *Oath*, and *Marriage-Covenant*, they will find and feel the blow of the Curse mentioned in Deut. 29.20, 21, 25. O what a fearful fire and fury, what dreadful death and damnation, is here threatened by the God of truth against them that break *his Covenant!* By which it is fully evident, that it is the duty of Wives to manifest their subjection to their Husbands, according to their Marriage-Covenant.

4. If Wives are not willing to subject themselves to the authority of their Husbands, it is because they do not really love them as God commands them. Tit. 2.4, 5. *That they may teach the young women to be sober, to love their Husbands, etc. to be obedient to their own Husbands, that the word of God be not blasphemed. God gives this injunction, that the Wife's love must proceed from the obedience of the Scripture:* And where the Wife loves her Husband in sincerity, there will be an orderly subjection of the Wife to the superiority of her Husband. When the Wife questions the Husband's right of superiority, she hath little love to his person; for Obedience is the evidence of love, and such Wives will honor their Husband's authority, who always look upon their persons and actions through the spectacles of love. But the Wife doth practically disown her Husband's authority over her, that neglects to observe the lawful commands of her Husband, or doth oppose him in doing lawful actions, or gives him imperious and insulting language. If a Wife doth really love her Husband, her yoke of *subjection* will not be grievous to her. As love to God doth exceedingly sweeten his service, and make it not only more acceptable to him, but also more delightful to us, as the Apostle saith, 1 Joh. 5.3. So the Wife's love to her Husband will abundantly sweeten her *subjection* to him. But if a Wife refuseth to give *subjection* to her Husband, and would be equal with him, or superior to him, she loves him not at

all. Let the Wife pretend what she will for neglecting the manifestations of her love to her Husband, by submission to his authority over her by God's institution, as the want of discretion, breeding, and other good qualities, which other Husbands have, or had: I must tell such a Wife, That not the good disposition of Husbands, or their excellent accomplishments, but the good pleasure of God, ought to be the ground of Wives' love to their Husbands, which they must evidence by an observance of all their lawful injunctions, and then they will do them good and not evil all the days of their lives, as in Prov. 31.12. By performing the several duties of their places, by honoring their persons, and submitting to their lawful pleasure. Some Wives murmur at the yoke of subjection, but truly they have more cause to complain of their want of affection; for women that love their Husbands will count their moderate commands, and whatsoever they do for them, both easy and delightful. If then, O Wife, thou canst say, *That thou hast chosen thy Husband for thy Love*, then love thy choice, and grudge not to submit thy self to his authority. Now this being granted, *That the Husband is the Wife's Superior*, I shall give Wives these following cautions in admonishing their Husbands of their sins and miscarriages.

1. Let Wives beware they do not pretend cause to reprove their Husbands out of a desire to usurp that authority to themselves which is due to their Husbands. Many think their Husbands deserve reproof for not carefully observing their wills: They look for obedience in everything from their Husbands, and think them guilty of a great crime if they do in any wise neglect to gratify their perverse humors. But I say, 'tis not the crossing of the Wife's pettish humor, but God's will, that deserves reproof. Some Wives account their Husbands denying them the liberty of disposing all Family-concerns according to their own pleasure,

to be a crime that deserves a smart reproof: They must rule all things, and manage all things themselves, or else the house will be too hot for their Husbands to abide in. Such Husbands deserve to be pitied whose outward beings by such Wives have been made as miserable as possible on this side Hell. The true ground of many Wives exclamations against their Husbands is a conceit that they do not rule enough, they think they are too much opposed in their wills. *O they cry out of such as vile Husbands as will not let them say what they will, and do what they will.* Many Women are noted for questioning and quarrelling at their Husbands' power, but few are noted for obeying their Husbands' pleasure. Therefore you Wives that may read this Treatise, consider with yourselves, whether you have not been offended with your Husbands, and pretended cause to manifest your displeasure against your Husbands, because your proud spirits are not willing to be in that subjection God hath placed you, and because you'd exercise an authority above your places, and so will pretend faults in your Husbands to justify your own presumptuous reprehensions of them, that so you might make them stoop to your humors; and if they do not, they shall have no quiet in their Families. Indeed this is a very great evil in Wives, and highly provoking to God, and they sin in reproving their Husbands on such an account. Therefore I would caution Wives to beware that they do not find fault with their Husbands upon such a ground: And to enforce this caution, I pray observe,

1. *That a commanding insulting Wife, who saith to her Husband,* you shall do this, *or* you shall not do it, *inverts the Order of Nature, as well as that of the Creator.*

2. *That a Family is infamous where the Wife like Jezabel rules all, and the Husband like Ahab lets her do what she list without contradiction. Where the Wife gets the upper-hand of the Hus-*

band, the next thing that is to be expected is an eclipse of the honor of that house.

3. Consider if you pretend cause to reprove your Husband's because they would keep you in subjection to them, according to God's command, you do not make conscience of rendering obedience to God. 'Tis not a sufficient excuse for a Wife to say, He doth not love me, therefore I will not obey him; *for not the Husbands affections to her, but her affection to God, must be her great motive to subjection. If the Husband fails in his duty, the Wife suffers by it: but if she fails in her duty to him, she sins in it; the former is a Cross to the Wife, but the latter is a Curse to her. Indeed when women pretend reason to reprove their Husbands because they do not willingly submit to their insulting over them, they do provoke God exceedingly; for God doth not in the least approve of such fond foolish Husbands, who deliver up that dominion which God hath given them, and suffer their Wives to trample over it, and trample upon it. In suffering themselves thus to be trampled upon, they suffer the Image and Glory of God to be trampled upon; their submission to their Wives' insulting is not kindness but baseness, not humility but iniquity. He unmans himself, who consents to be ruled by one whom he should rule, and he must expect to be accountable for it to God. Therefore, I say, you that are Wives look well to the ground that moves you to acquaint your Husband of any miscarriage, see that it be not the effect of a proud insulting humor, out of a desire to exercise dominion over them, nor the effect of a passionate, peevish humor, by way of revenge, because your wills are crossed, or that your corrupt fancies are not indulged.*

2. Beware you do not chide your Husbands, instead of admonishing them, for, I say, it is always unlawful for a Wife to chide her Husband at any time, for anything, for the person chiding, according to the nature of the act, takes superiority over the party chided, whereby the Wife breaks God's order, and contradicts his Word, thereby showing only the sad effects of a furious spirit, manifesting that fire of pride rageth in her, which is always accompanied with fire of contention. Therefore the Wife when she speaks to her Husband of miscarriages, she must do it in the most humble manner that she can, she must always do it by way of entreaty and humble desire. When you would admonish your Husbands of their sins, or advise them about their spiritual estates, first beg God's direction in, and blessing on, what you are about to do, then in the particular, close dealing with an Husband about the evil of his way, humbly, meekly, and mildly tell him, *that such a particular practice is against such a particular Scripture*. Then entreat him humbly, persuade him affectionately, beseech him earnestly, woe him as for your life, that if possible (through God's blessing) you prevail with him to alter his practice. But many women, instead of taking this course, scold at their Husbands, speak harshly, frowardly, and revilingly to them: Yet assuredly nothing more raiseth the passions of an Husband, than the irreverent, rude, audacious carriage, and chiding language of a Wife, whereby she usurps authority over him. Thus Zipporah carried it to her Husband Moses, who was a man of God, the meekest man on earth, she gave him harsh, chiding, and reviling language, for observing what God commanded, Exod. 4.25. *Surely a bloody Husband thou art to me*. Truly such Wives as presume to chide their Husbands, are of an Ethiopian spirit. Chiding words are a great offense to an Husband, and if continued by the Wife upon every trifling occasion, will have a mighty tendency to abate affection. For such an unbecoming carriage of a Wife, under a pretense of admonition, doth but deny reverence and subjection to the Husband; for if Wives tell their Husbands of their faults in an insolent way, using hard and bitter words, and a sour fretting countenance, they may provoke them, but not reform them. Therefore, O Wives, be not so arrogant as to chide your Husbands, who by their superiority have right to chide you when you miscarry. And chiding can never be termed admonishing, when 'tis done by an inferior to a Superior, but rather an arrogant insulting. Indeed when inferiors chide their Superiors, they are not like by so doing to effect a work of conviction on them, they may be instrumental of raising their passions, but not of prevailing with them to acknowledge their sins. Let not Wives then presume to chide their Husbands whom they are bound humbly to entreat. But when they speak to their Husbands, or of their Husbands, let it be with a great deal of respect.

3. Beware you do not ground your admonitions upon false interpretations of your Husband's actions, and judging them to perform good actions from an evil principle, to a sinful end. By this means many Wives have reviled and reproached their Husbands exceedingly. This was Michal's fault, she irreverently rebuked David, or rather reviled him, f*or rejoicing before the Lord at the bringing home of the Ark.* She chargeth him for *carrying of himself like a vain fellow, undervaluing himself, and doing that which was beneath his quality, doing as fools used to do when they are hired to make sport.* David might seem to some to be very tart in his reply to his Wife, in 2 Sam. 6.21. Indeed David had just cause to be thus sharp, not only because the flouts and insolencies of a Wife are most unsufferable, but especially because it was his Zeal and Devotion in the service of God which she derided. I have heard of a woman that was so vile as to censure her Husband, that when he had set a day apart to humble himself before the Lord in the sense of his sin, she told him, (without anything done or said by him to raise her choler) *That he had kept a Fast to the Devil.* And what is the reason that Michal and other Women thus mis-

interpret their Husbands' actions, and revile their persons, under a pretense of reproving their faults? They did not enter into the conjugal relation purely out of love to their persons: there was something else that influenced them thereunto, which they were frustrated in, and so they do as Michal did, 1 Chron. 15.29. *she despised him in her heart*. This is the great cause of women's unbecoming carriages to their Husbands, and indeed God will deal severely with such Wives, as he did with Michal: *She had no child until the day of her death*. Because of this wickedness, God adjudged her to perpetual barrenness, which was a great reproach at that time. Such as have their Husbands contemptible in their eyes, God will make them contemptible in every eye: God will either by barrenness deprive them of having Children, or (that which is a greater affliction) let them have weak and sickly children, which he will quickly take from them by death or let their Children prove a scourge or curse to them. *O Wives! you will first charge your Husbands falsely with faults from a rash, envious and wicked misinterpreting their actions, and then pretend cause to reprove them, when the fault you charge them with is of your own forging, Therefore, O Wives! you must carefully beware that you do not charge your Husbands with any miscarriages from your own malicious wresting of the sense of their words or actions; for in this you offend God highly. There are few Wives but will pretend reasons for finding fault with their Husbands, when they can evidence none; and their contentious wranglings are the effects of putting false constructions upon their words and actions, conceiting things to be otherwise than in truth they are, and upon this ground they have presumed to carry it irreverently to their Husbands. I say, they must take care of miscarrying in this respect.*

    4. You must not presume to admonish your Husbands for anything but that which tends to destroy his Soul, or impoverish

his Family: that is, for that which is a dishonor to God, a breach of his Law, a straying from the Divine Rule, or a neglect of the duty that God requires from them; or (2dly.) a wasting of their Estates by misemploying or extravagantly consuming them, thereby not providing for the necessaries of their families. For lesser matters than these you are not to find fault with your Husbands at all: *as, for gestures of the body, for sometimes using the vulgar dialect of the Country in discourse, not keeping their apparel in that excellent order as some do, or the fashion requires, for not complementing, for not manifesting a fond carriage to you, for not telling you everything they are about to do before they act it, for not observing your times for staying at home or going abroad, for discoursing with persons of an inferior quality, you thinking it too much beneath them, some innocent actions of the hand in talking, or such inconsiderable trifles that are not in their own nature sinful.* I say, such things you are not to take notice of in your Husbands, nor manifest yourselves angry with your Husbands for them. A truly gracious Soul can very well bear with such trifles in an Husband without being distasted with him, and such Wives as cannot do either evidence the weakness of their grace, or their want of grace. But there are some Wives of such wrangling spirits, as that they will use more violent expressions in finding fault with such trifles, than at any time they will do when their Husbands sin against God Though they ought in a limited sense and due manner to admonish them of the sins that they do commit, yet the Wife may not at any time lawfully reprove the Husband for that which is not sinful, yet she may humbly desire him to comply with her in things indifferent if he think fit. But for a Wife to contend with an Husband about inconsiderable toys, is very unbecoming her, and the cause of much disquiet in a Family. Many Wives are apt to censure that to be sin in an Husband, which is not; as I can instance in one, that looked upon *the sighs and groans of her Husband, and the rising and falling of his voice in Prayer, to be hypocrisy, affectation, and self-conceitedness*; when, for ought she knew, they might be the effects and evidences of fervency in spirit: as in Rom. 8.26. *We know not what we should pray for, but the Spirit it self maketh intercession for us with groanings which cannot be uttered*: that is, the Spirit helpeth us to make us earnest and fervent in prayer, which is evidenced by groanings, beyond what can be evidenced by the bare expression of the mouth; yea, groanings do evidence an ardent desire of mind, even when we are not able to speak; and indeed that prayer which is breathed in and out by the Spirit of God, cannot be without some external evidences, either of voice countenance, or sighs. Do not then condemn that prayer which may be of the spirits working, and indeed were we more fervent in prayer, we should manifest more sighings and groanings in it. Prayer is not to be measured by the multitude and fineness of words, but by the earnest groans of the heart. Sighs and groans evidence more of the heart in prayer, than words alone; for words alone may be but babbling, and as the drawing nigh of the hypocrite. Considering this, let no woman find fault with that in an Husband, which the word of God doth not condemn in him. Though many of his carriages may not please her humor, yet she must patiently bear with them, and not speak against them, except they be sinful, and she can prove them so by Scripture. It is better by much to be silent, than to cry out against that which we cannot prove to be sin by God's word. No good is done by reproving a deed, except by Scripture the doer can be convinced of sin.

5. Be careful that under pretense of reproving your Husbands, you do not utter any expressions that tend to the undervaluing and contempt of your Husbands' persons, parts or education; for reproachful and disgraceful words given to an Husband,

will cause conjugal affections to decay very much. If you reproach your Husbands when you pretend to reprove their sins, you will break their heads instead of their hearts, and make them fly in your faces, instead of falling down at God's feet. Some are apt to manifest their dislike of being related to their Husbands, as their Wives, and this is very sinful, nay it is sinful to wish so in their hearts, for therein they quarrel at the providence, and dislike the appointments of God. Some will say to their Husbands when they are at any time crossed in their humors, *If I had known this and this by thee before, as well as I do now, I would never have had thee for my Husband.* Some Wives will drop expressions as if they deserved a better Husband than they had, one richer and better than they had. Some will tell their Husbands, *They had better married some inferior person which would have better suited their clownish breeding than with them who were better educated.* All which expressions tend to the undervaluing their Husbands' persons and education, and such Wives who by their carriages and expressions do thus slight their Husbands, are never like to convince them of sin; they may perplex and afflict them, but not do them good. Some men are more troubled with what is said to them, than what is done to them. Unfriendly and undervaluing speeches have lain heavier upon them, than the heaviest of pressures. *Job was broken in pieces with words*, chap. 19.2. Indeed reproachful and reviling language hath occasioned many sad effects, for cruel words many times provoke to cruel actions. Hard words are numbered amongst the hardest trials. *If then, O Wife, under a pretense of reproving thy Husband's sin, thou dost reproach him, and speak undervaluingly of him, thou endeavorest to make him a shame and reproach to evil men, but not make him ashamed of any sin: and indeed such reproachings will make and increase breaches between you; and such Husbands must have their senses stupefied, that can bear such carriages from a Wife. When offenders are reproved, it is to make them ashamed, not to shame them; but those are reproaches, and not rebukes, that make men a shame, and not ashamed. But indeed if thou dost endeavor to cast contempt on thy Husband, notwithstanding thou may'st be a Professor, it is an evidence that he is gracious, and thou art carnal, for none receive more contempt on earth, than they whose names are written in Heaven. Such as are wicked cannot but despise those who are in esteem with God.* I knew a professor of Religion, that when her Husband was speaking something of no great concern, he speaking but one word more than she thought fit or seasonable, she fell into such a rage, that she said *he was worse than the Devil of Hell*, and yet pleaded in her justification, *She must speak against sin, and that he was a vile fellow and she could not make him worse than he was*; and yet she could not say that anything he spoke was sinful. But Though some Wives in their passions speak to and of their Husbands as if they were the vilest of men, yet when God doth visit them with a violent fit of sickness, or any other sore affliction, they will sometimes acknowledge that they have wronged them, and desire them to pardon their unbecoming carriage towards them. 'Tis sad when such as are no relations do revile and reproach a man, and speak contemptibly of him: but 'tis more sad to be reviled and reproached by a Wife, and no reason or pretense that she can bring can possibly excuse her so doing. 'Tis a grief to hear those that are vile revile and throw dirt in their faces, whose faces shine through that beauty and comeliness which God hath put upon them: but to see a Wife throw dirt in the face of her Husband who is gracious, and bespatter and bemire his credit, is very sad and lamentable, neither can the vileness that the Wife may pretend to be in her Husband, if he were really as bad as she asserts him to be, justify her in reviling of him; for the Husband's faultiness is no good plea for the Wife's miscarriage. God doth permit many gracious Husbands to be thus reviled by their Wives, to exercise their graces, that their patience may have its perfect work, and that they may not idolize such Relations. Indeed such Wives as drop expressions tending to the undervaluing of their Husbands, by speaking contemptibly of them, they loathe their very persons. I heard of one, (and I suppose I knew her) that said to her Husband, *Thou art a stinking fellow, I cannot bear the smell of thy breath 'tis so offensive, unpleasant, noisome, and ill-savory to me.* So her Husband might complain as Job did, chap 19.17. *My breath was strange to my Wife*: that is, did seem loathsome to my Wife. First, that which moved upon his breath, his word or voice, his speech or complaint. Words are nothing but breath formed and shaped to express our minds by: so then *my breath was strange* (that is, my words, my complaints) to her; my discourses with her are strange, she will not hear me speak, my voice is offensive and unpleasant to her. Secondly, take breath for that which we respire or breathe forth while we live, that is loathsome and unsavory to her, as unsavory meat which the stomach loatheth, and cannot digest. Yet I must tell you the virtue of some Wives have appeared gloriously, that when diseases have made all others loathe their Husbands, they have delighted in them; and while true conjugal love lives, there will be no contempt of one another's persons, no loathing one another for any bodily imperfections. But indeed this same woman that loathed Husband's breath, did in Job 2.9 bid him *curse God, and die.* Truly then her breath was strange to him, because 'twas a sinful breath. And such as by any ways manifest a contempt of their Husbands have such a principle in them as Job's Wife had; therefore beware that under pretense of reproving your Husbands you do not speak revilingly to them.

6. Be careful that under pretense of finding fault with your Husband's miscarriages, you do not reveal your Husband's weaknesses unto others, but hide their infirmities as much as you can. Whatever right you have to admonishing your Husbands, certainly you have no right to do it before others: for then you will divulge their failings to others, which by no means you ought to do; neither would you ever presume to do it, if you had dear love for them, f*or charity covereth many infirmities*, 1 Pet. 4.8. And so in Prov. 11.13. *A talebearer revealeth secrets, but he that is of a faithful spirit concealeth the matter.* So in Prov. 10.12. *True charity hath a garment long and large enough to cover many, yea, a multitude of sins.* Charity ought to cover the sins of others as to the preservation of their credit amongst men. So then while you are admonishing or wisely reproving your Husbands, you ought to conceal their faults from others, and not to publish and blaze them abroad to their shame, or to the Provocation of Passion in them and it is a great piece of Christian Wisdom so to do, and may be a means of recovering them from the Power and practice of their Sins. O Wives! you many times talk of the Actions of your Husbands, to make sport for your Company, and say you meant no hurt, you did it only in jest, and by way of diversion, or to make him ashamed of his indiscreet Actions, I say such discoverings of your Husbands' Actions are directly sinful and your relating of any failings or hasty inconsiderate expressions of your Husbands unto others, will make all your just and lawful Admonitions ineffectual. You must be careful therefore not to utter anything of your Husband's unto others that may blemish their Reputations, prejudice or undervalue their Persons. But if your Husbands are obstinate or perverse in their sins; or continue in such Actions as the Scripture asserts to be sinful, so that your lawful endeavors cannot reclaim them, or that their carriages to you, are unchris-

tian-like, that you are in a kind of bondage and slavery with them that they do oppress you, take Vicious Courses; Consume their Estates, and neglect to provide necessaries for you contrary to the Gospel Rule, then you may acquaint your Godly Minister or Pastor, or some prudent judicious Christian Friend, that will keep your Counsel, whom you may desire to confer with your Husbands, and endeavor to convince them of the evil of their ways, and persuade them to carry it more affectionately towards you. But you must divulge their failings in a common way, you may as soon undergo God's Curse for discovering your Husbands' nakedness as your Parents', for your Husbands are nearer Relations to you, than your Parents. Therefore if you would do good to your Husbands by any advice and counsel that you do respectfully give them, do not publish their failings unto others.

    7. If you would reclaim your Husbands from any evil way to a faithful walking in the ways of God, your orderly and regular Conversation is the most effectual means of gaining them, and winning upon them, 1 Pet. 3.1, 2. *Likewise ye wives be in subjection to your own husbands, that if any obey not the word, they also may without the word be won by the conversation of the wives, which they behold your chaste conversation coupled with fear.* By this means they might by God's blessing prevail with their Husbands to conform to the Gospel Rule, when they can mark nothing but chastity and holiness to their Wives' Conversations. Now winning Conversation doth consist,

    1. In a Reverend Esteem of the Husband, as one placed by the Lord in a degree of Superiority above her. Likewise ye Wives be in Subjection to your own Husbands, for know that the Sin of an Husband doth not exempt the Wife from her duty, but rather tie her the more strictly to the duty of Subjection. Wicked Husbands observing the dutiful carriage of their Wives to them, not-

withstanding they have been very unkind to their Wives, will be brought to believe some excellency in Religion, that doth enable them so to do, so by degrees attain a liking of Religion, and endeavor to be Religious.

2. A chaste Conversation coupled with Fear, as in the second Verse, there is no part of a Christian's Conversation so prevalent to gain others to fall in love with Religion, as that wherein the duties we owe to others in the Relation we have to them do shine; for these two; first, Chastity which is the main duty in Reference to the manifesting of the faithfulness of the Wife to the Husband; and fear which signifies the Reverence the Wife owes to the Husband as her Superior, whereby she is afraid to displease him. These I say are the qualities of a Christian Conversation which the spirit of God condescends to intimate, as most prevalent to gain Evil Husbands to fall in Love with Religion. When an Husband observes the modesty, chastity and faithfulness of his Wife, the care she hath to please him in all lawful things, and her watchfulness to avoid everything that may distaste him. It will influence him very much to like Religion, which prompts her to such an obliging Conversation.

3. In order to attaining this winning conversation, whereby Wives might reclaim their Husbands from sin by their outward carriages, they should take great care to attain a right frame of Spirit, *to have their inward man adorned with meekness and peaceableness of spirit*, as in 1 Pet. 3.4. This is the way for Wives to commend Religion unto their Husbands, and to win them to fall in love with it by their outward carriages. Their prime care must be exercised to manifest in life and practice that their hearts are adorned with the graces of God's Spirit, then their conversations cannot but be lovely to their Husbands. This is the way of gaining such a conversation, as will gain their Husbands to an holy life.

Now those graces in a Wife, that have the most powerful Influence to prevail upon her Husband are Meekness and Quietness of Spirit.

    1. Meekness whereby she keeps down her passions from rising against her Husband, Though he wrongs her, or against the Lord's dispensations in exercising her more hardly than others, whereby she useth all amicable and loving ways to reclaim her Husband from continuing to deal injuriously with her.

    2. Quietness of Spirit whereby she doth eschew all needless contradictions of her Husband, all rashness in her Actions, all meddling with things not belonging to her, all expressions of discontent with that lot which the Lord hath carved out to her, and such carriages of a Wife will work more upon an Husband's heart than the strongest Arguments and sharpest Reproofs she can assault him with. Now the Apostle doth enforce this Exhortation to Wives with these two Arguments. The first is taken from the example of holy believing Women, who counted it their best Ornament to manifest their Holiness and Faith by their dutifulness to their Husbands, and particularly of Sarah who testified her Obedience and Subjection to her Husband, by her Respectful and Reverend carriage towards him, and language to him. *She obeyed him and called him Lord*, 1 Pet. 3.6. The second Argument is from the advantage of such a carriage, and such a winning Conversation, that if they did imitate these Holy Women, especially Sarah in dutifulness to her Husband, notwithstanding any wrongs they might receive from them, they should prove themselves Heirs of Sarah's blessedness. So when we obtain Grace from the Lord to follow the Footsteps of the Saints Registered in the Scripture, especially in the Faithful discharge of the duties of our particular Stations and Relations, then do we prove ourselves to have a right to be made partakers of the same spiritual privileges with them;

and Heirs of the same Eternal Blessedness which they now possess. So Wives behaving themselves to their Husbands in a Dutiful, Respectful, Reverential way, manifesting a chaste Conversation coupled with fear, having their hearts in a gracious frame adorned with meekness and quietness of spirit, they will clear up to themselves their right to Sarah's Blessedness, and enjoy the sense of their interest in the spiritual privileges that she had; and by their meek and quiet Conversations be very prevalent to win their Husbands from the error of their ways. When God by the Spirit hath hushed the storms and tempests that usually arise in the Spirits of Wives, when he breaths upon them with a favorable wind, and stills their Spirits, and restrains Satan the master of misrule, that he doth not kindle Jealousies and Animosities in their Spirits, but that they have a spiritual quietness of heart and tranquility of mind wrought in them by the sweet breathings of the blessed spirit, which they can retain when they have the highest Provocations from their Husbands to unquietness; then they will have a mighty influence upon their Husbands, to reclaim them from their Vicious Actions and violent passions. Although the Children of the Lord be bound to deal with those with whom they live or converse, that they observe to sin by discourse and conference, commending Christ to them, and opening the evil of sin to them, and their dangerous State if they remain impenitent, the necessity of reforming their lives and entertaining Christ in their hearts by faith: Yet it is mainly a Conversation suitable to the word of God, that God useth to bless to make men fall in love with Religion, without which the best discourse will rather harden them in sin, than reclaim them from their sinful ways. Then I say do Wives stop the mouths of their Husbands, when their conversations for Piety unto God, and Righteousness unto them is such as may discover unto their Husbands their failings, and point out unto them that good way wherein they ought to walk, for the Wife's sweet calmness of spirit, and pleasant serenity of mind prevails to restrain her from all tart expressions and bitter words, and to forbear all exasperating language, and enables her to bear reviling language with patience, without rendering reviling for reviling; yea without answering again in a froward way; which carriage doth so convince a froward and unruly Husband, that he is by the blessing of God powerfully influenced to comply with the counsels of his Wife. O let Wives shine as lights in the world, holy, blameless, and harmless, and by their practice hold forth the word of life unto their Husbands, so that by a suitable practice joined with their professions, Wives will be the same to their Husbands in order to their conviction, discovery of their Sin, and manifesting the lovely beauty of the ways of holiness, as the Sun and Moon is in the Firmament discovering things hidden by natural darkness 1 Pet. 2.15, 16. And indeed this is the principal way that wives can lawfully take to help on the Reformation of their Husbands. This I say is their most proper course, and will help on their Husbands' amendment, when harsh biting and smart words will make them worse both to God and them. Indeed the Wife's best Counsel will signify nothing to the Husband's good without a regular, meek and quiet Conversation. Therefore in order to the persuading of an Husband from sin let the Wife take care to order her Conversation aright. Consider then O Wives: have you cause to complain, that none of your endeavors have proved effectual in order to your Husbands' Reformation? But have you not taken a wrong Method to effect it? Have you not manifested too much bitterness in speaking against your Husbands' failings? have you not manifested too much rage and violence when they have crossed your humor in some domestic concerns? Have you not spoken to them in a fierce, furious and irreverent manner? Then blame your own passions as the cause of your Husbands' Obstinacy, were you more mild and respectful in your carriages to them, they would be more complying with you, if you would then do them good by your advice, advise them in an humble and meek way.

8. If you would do your Husbands good by your Admonitions, be careful that you never admonish them, but when they are in a good mood or very pleasant humor, if a work be not done in a proper season, it were better not done at all, when you find them in a good temper, as sometimes the worst of men will be, then manifest the dear affection that you have for them, tell them what tender regard you have for their Eternal good, their present Reputation and Comfort. Then use such persuasive arguments, as may be most taking with their Constitutions, still carrying yourselves with all due respect and submission to their Authority over you, and if you cannot prevail with them to Reform, then when you find them alone; tell them once again of their faults in an humble, modest and meek manner, even weeping, as the Apostle spoke to the Philippians, Chap. 3.18. *And now I tell you even weeping*, this hath proved a most effectual and prevailing way when all other means have failed.

But it is strange to see what Violence and Fury of Spirit some do manifest under pretense of reproving their Husbands' miscarriages. If their Husbands do but walk abroad about their lawful occasions, even such as concern the providing for the maintenance of their Families, if they have any frivolous matters that they fancy to employ them about, which doth not in the least belong to them to be concerned in it must be done then, and only then, when their honest and lawful occasions do call them abroad, and then if their Husbands will not gratify them in laying aside their business to gratify their peevish insulting humors they will censure their going forth to be ungodly and devilish, and that they spend their time in ungodly Company, that they hope God will stop their going forth in a short time, and wish that they were some way smitten of God to be constrained to stay within, and continue their reviling language as long as they abide in company with them, sometime asserting them to be Hypocrites, at other times, assert them to be Profane, and all this such Wives do because their Husbands will not be as Subject to them as an Apprentice is to his Master, they will complain if they have not all things according to their mind, and yet storm at their Husbands, using lawful endeavors to provide them. If their Husbands have no business abroad, How are they provided for? How have they a supply of all things necessary for their maintenance? they cannot prove their Husbands keep bad Company, or that they are frequenters of Taverns, or Ale-Houses, or concerned in extravagant Expenses, yet talk to them, and of them no otherwise then as to, and of a Rogue that is going from Newgate to Tyburne, I appeal to all the Professors of Religion in the Kingdom, whether they can conceive any Grace to be in the Hearts of such Wives, and whether they do not carry themselves as such as are acted by some infernal Fury. Let them pretend what they will, and if in truth their Husbands were as vile as their furious Tongues do declare, yet they cannot Justify their present carriages, nor justify the Omission of manifesting that Respect and Reverence which according to God's word they owe them, as they are their Husbands, so long as the Relation continues their Relational Duties continue, and they ought to submit to their Husbands' superiority, though it doth not please them. Therefore let not Wives pretend that to be done in Zeal for God, which is but disgorging the scum and froth a furious Spirit.

    But there are many gracious Wives who are not of this furious temper, but abhor such furious carriages, who live very comfortably with their Husbands, they are dutiful and respectful to their Husbands, and their Husbands are loving and kind to them, and they have much content and satisfaction, delight and complacency in each other. There are no contentions between them; what the Husband orders, the Wife cheerfully submits unto. She owns him for her head, for her guide, for her governor, and presumes not to insult over him, or contradict or control him, and by this means there is a sweet harmony between them, and they are Comforts and Blessings to each other.

I come now to the last particular, wherein I shall speak to both Husbands and Wives together, and persuade them to be more careful to carry themselves more Christianlike to their Children and Servants, which will be a special means to preserve peace and concord amongst themselves. Certainly one reason why Husbands and Wives do not live comfortably together, is their neglecting to give their Children a Pious Education, which through Divine assistance might be a special means to heal the vitiosity of their depraved natures, and to master and conquer their sinful propensions. God in judgment permits Husbands and Wives to be plagues to each other, who neglect by education to refine and reform their Children, and make them pliable to the Divine Will, who are rugged and untoward by nature; for if an Husband be not tender of a regular carriage to his inferiors, he will never be tender of a dutiful carriage to God. And if the Wife doth not carry herself as she ought to her Children and Servants, she will never carry herself as she ought towards her Husband, nor have any tender care to promote God's honor. If Husbands and Wives did better discharge their duties to their inferiors, they would live more peaceably with each other. Therefore I shall give them some directions how they should carry themselves to inferiors in general, and then give some particular directions how they ought to carry themselves to their Children in respect of instruction and correction.

1. *Concerning their carriage to inferiors in general.*

1. Let Husbands and Wives be careful not to be too hasty or sudden in charging faults on their Children, Servants, or other inferiors. For sudden surprises do put them by all due consideration, that many times they speak what otherwise they would not. Therefore give them time to consider what to answer, and advise them to speak the truth though against themselves, telling them, *That a lie will double their fault, and greatly increase their guilt.*

2. In reproving your inferiors, manage your reproofs so prudently that you may manifest *love to their persons* when you evidence the *dislike of their sins*. Begin gently to use all persuasive motives to reclaim them from sin, and allure them to the ways of God. Never use severity but in cases of flat necessity, lest the too frequent exercise of severity make them to despise you, and harden them against you. When you mix some severe expressions of holy anger against their sin, let it be done in a grave prudent way; for when you deal with them in a boisterous way, you only put them into a slavish fear. Let them perceive that you are more displeased with them for offenses committed directly against God, than yourselves. Pray let not your passions, like *unruly torrents*, overflow the banks that are limited by Scripture and Reason. A grave carriage, and a sober moderate anger, will procure reverence, and advance reformations; but that which is mixed with horrid noise and clamors, floweth from the breast of fools. A Child can never persuade himself that such anger proceedeth from love, when he is made the sink to receive the daily disgorgements of a choleric stomach, when the unhappy necessity of his relation ties him to be always in the way, where an angry disposition must vent and empty itself. If you that rule be thus unruly, how can you expect

your inferiors to be regular, when your uncomely demeanor doth almost convince them that love can hardly be the genuine root of your anger, but that they are made the sad objects of your native temper, and that your reprehensions are spiced with hatred. If you have cause to be angry, yet let not your storms run all upon the Rocks, but endeavor speedily to cool the inflammation, to abate the fever, and slack the fire of your anger.

3. Observe a prudent administration of your rebukes, gild those bitter Pills with hopes of winning your favor upon their amendment, mix those unpleasant potions with some sweet emollient Juices that such interwoven lenity may procure access for your admonitions, and effect your desired issue: Great and heinous faults, if repeated, deserve a greater ardency of spirit. Smaller offenses of Wife, Children, and Servants, if they be not committed openly, rebuke them apart and in private: Wink at infirmities and failings that are not positively sinful in a plain breach of the known Law of God. Reserve your severest and sharpest reprehensions for open and scandalous sins that have been reiterated, having a show of contempt and disdain, 1 Tim. 5.20.

4. Beware that you do not reprove your inferiors to gratify a froward and perverse humor. Your aims and intentions must be upright in reproving. Take heed of mingling any wildfire of pride, vainglory, and ambitious humor of contradicting and controlling others, with your zeal of reproving. Let your rebukes be purely for God's glory, out of hatred unto sin, and out of love to the Salvation of your inferiors.

5. If you would reform the miscarriages of your inferiors; do it by way of instruction and preceptive injunctions. Lay it as a charge upon their souls in the name of God, *That they hearken to and obey your institutions*. Efficacious words, rather than many, are to be sought, studied and used. There be some, especially Wives,

when they are displeased with their Children or Servants, when they begin to speak against what they dislike, they are not willing to give over, but keep thundering out their frivolous repetitions of the same things for an hour together. Therefore beware when you reprove the faults of inferiors, that you do not multiply words, for in a multitude of words, there will be many impertinencies which nourish contentions, and rather bring contempt upon the reprover, than reform the reproved. Therefore in few words and insignificant terms, enjoin them to conform to your instructions that you give them from God's word, and say no more, but with a grave look dismiss them.

 6. Before your reprove your inferiors, or join corrections with your reproofs, consider, *Whither their faults proceed from imprudence and weakness, or obstinacy and willfulness? upon what grounds and occasions, upon what provocations and seductions?* and deal with them according to the circumstances their faults are clothed with: If they appear to be truly sorrowful and deeply humbled, and do readily beg forgiveness of God and you, with a promise of amendment, and leading a new life, you ought to deal gently with them.

 7. *Take heed of exasperating and provoking Wives, Children and Servants by rigid and severe courses, where less may affect your purpose. There are some cruel Husbands and Wives that carry themselves more like raging Bruits, than men and women, that take pleasure in tyrannical corrections. If they do not act what they would have them, as they would have them, and as soon as they would have them, they fall upon those their inferiors, and tare them like wild beasts. Such Superiors are apt to interpret their inferiors' actions in the worst sense and say they are faulty in their actions because they hate their persons, and so deal rigidly and hardly with them. Take heed of making your Wives, Children and Servants vile*

in your eyes by too much severity, and know that God will require such vile acts at your hands at the great day.

8. Though you ought to maintain the eminency of your places above your inferiors, though you ought to order and manage your actions with such gravity as may gain some awe and respect from their hearts, and though you ought to uphold the honor and preeminence of that station wherein God hath set you, by all prudent means: yet you must not carry yourselves towards your inferiors with any proud, supercilious or fastuous deportment. As you need not indent your cheeks with continual smiles, so neither plow your foreheads with rough and sour wrinkles. A sober affability and unaffected and amiable gravity, will sufficiently chastise contempt, and nourish a reverend love. Rigid austerity in words and actions will produce a slavish dispirited temper in Children and Servants, that when they come to years they are so pusillanimous, that they are rendered unfit to manage the work of their Generation. The dogged carriages of your Superiors, with a word and a blow to Children and Servants upon every trifling occasion, works in them an over-much rustic slavery, makes them dejected, dull, and stupid, and unfit for any service. Carry yourselves therefore in that manner, that they may neither fear or have your morosity, nor grow wanton upon the commonness of your carriage.

9. Be careful not to manifest too much severity against a fault when 'tis ingeniously and fully confessed, for if you do, you will cause your Children and Servants to deny the truth another time. When Superiors are equally severe when their inferiors confess, as when they deny the truth of the fact, they provoke them to lie. If a confession of a fault doth not procure a moderation of correction, yea sometimes an omission of correction, another time inferiors will obstinately deny what they have done, and add sin to sin. And let such superiors know, that they are guilty of every such lie their infe-

riors tell, and shall answer for it as their own sin.

I have here given those general directions how Husbands and Wives should carry themselves to their inferiors, because their disorderly carriages to Children and Servants have caused hot contests between them. When the one hath fallen fiercely upon a Child or Servant, the other hath disliked it, and thereupon have fallen out with each other, and have been so furious against each other, that they have not been reconciled in a long time. Therefore, O Husbands and Wives, as you desire to have a comfortable enjoyment of each other, observe those directions in your carriages to your inferiors.

But I pass on to the next particular, *to give some particular directions to Husbands and Wives concerning the education of their Children.*

1. Beware of manifesting your affections to one Child more than another, but show equal love to them all, otherwise that will be an heinous crime in one, which will seem no blemish or fault in the other. For an unequal affection blinds the judgment, and the child that is not respected, is dealt harsher with, whereby it is very much discouraged, dejected, and grieved.

2. Do not overmuch restrain them from innocent and lawful recreations but give them some convenient liberty to refresh themselves in the exercise of them, which may better dispose them to receive benefit by your education, and be a means the sooner to make your godly instructions to them.

3. Beware of base vilifying language in your rebukes, which will provoke Children to be dogged, sullen, and grow worse rather than reform them.

4. Do you sometimes wink at small things in Children, and not chide them for every trifle, else as Children grow older, Parents will grow contemptible.

5. Let not the Mother chide or correct the Child in the Father's presence; but if the Father doth not observe the present ill behavior, or know of a former miscarriage, let the Wife then inform the Husband, whose right then it is to chide or correct by the authority of his place, or deal with the Child when the Father is gone forth, for otherwise she doth not respect her Husband's superiority over herself as well as the Child.

6. Use not many words in rebuking your Children. Let your words be few, proper and weighty, and let your carriage be grave, but not fierce.

7. Do not upbraid your Children with former miscarriages in your passionate heats, for which they have received reproof and correction before, but when the same faults are again renewed, give new reproofs or corrections, as the nature of the offense doth require.

8. Study the constitutions of your Children. Mildness will do better with some, than severity, and the dispositions of others need severity to be exercised towards them.

9. When the Husband rebukes a Child, let the Wife be silent, and not plead for him in the child's hearing: If the Husband doth what is not proper, let her tell him of it in private.

10. If you are angry with Children for some miscarriage, forbear rebuking or correcting, till your spirits are cooled. That cannot be done regularly that is done in fury. Whatever is done rashly will be done disorderly, and so no good effect can be produced.

11. Be careful that you be not causers of your children's' undutifulness and disobedience by your bad examples and ill behavior. If you have not walked so circumspectly as the duties of your Children might be due unto you, even in regard of your behavior you have brought on yourselves the guilt of your Chil-

dren's want of duty. You should be holy, grave and modest in your lives, and eminently exemplary for practical godliness, and then your instructions will more effectually influence their hearts, and breed and continue in them an awe and reverence of your parental authority. But alas! in how many places are Parents of careless and loose lives, of peevish and froward humors, betraying their neglect of Religion, going to Religious Exercises when they list, making every trifling occasion a sufficient excuse for neglecting Christian duties, sometimes pretending inability of body, when laziness and want of affection is the principal cause of their neglects! Others carry no gravity in their doings, nor modesty in their behaviors, but live most dissolutely, and often incontinently. Others swear fearfully without regard, speaking profanely, not respecting the frailty of the youth that hear them. Sometimes Husbands and Wives let unkind speeches pass from them one towards another in the presence of their Children, to the great impairing of their credit with them. Other Parents are too careless of bringing up their Children *in the fear of God, in the nature and admonition of the Lord*, as they are bound Ephes. 6.4. All these are means to make Children fail in reverence to their Parents, and to tempt them to sin; and Though you may be grieved that your Children want a reverend regard of you, yet yourselves have been causers of the same. *Pray then consider. O ye Parents, what cause ye have given of your Children's disobedience, and bewail it, and be watchful against such carriages for the future, as have heretofore occasioned their disobedience; for surely what duties the Law bindeth all Children to perform, it as strictly bindeth all Parents to deserve. The Parents' evil doth not at all excuse the Child's miscarriages, but it maketh him guilty of his Child's offense. Beg then of God to pardon your past miscarriages, and to work such gracious principles in you, that you may never more be precedents in sin to your Children, that you may not by your bad examples draw them into the ways of their ruin. Your laboring by an holy life to deserve duty from your Children, will exceedingly forward your Children's performance of their duties in you. So that it is your great concern to beware of speaking or doing anything before your Children, that you would not have them to imitate you in; for Children are more forward to imitate the examples of their Parents in things that are evil, than in things that are good. Therefore be patterns of good to them, be patterns of meekness, and not of wrath, that they may observe that in your behaviors that deserves their imitation, and so may be followers of you in well doing. O that Parents would strictly observe those directions, that their Children may be piously educated, whereby they may be able to take comfort in their modest, respectful, and orderly behavior towards them.*

12. Abuse not your parental authority by provoking your Children to wrath, or by embittering their Spirits, Ephes. 6.4. And this is done,

1. *By denying them that which is their due, in Food, Raiment, or means of Education, neglecting to bring them up in an honest Calling, whereby they might get their living in the fear of God*, Lament. 4.3, 4.

2. *By commanding them to do things unjust in themselves, as in* 1 Sam. 20.31. *or by unjust and rigorous commands about things in their own nature indifferent,* 1 Sam. 14.28, 29. *You lay great burdens upon your Children, pressing them still with your authority. You enjoin them what you list, not weighing well what they like, and not carefully considering as well their natures, as your own desires, as well their comfort and convenient being, as your own affection and will to have it, whereby your Children's lives are very much embittered.*

3. *By inveighing with bitter words against them, giving*

them furious speeches and violent language, chiefly when there is no cause, as Saul did to Jonathan, 1 Sam. 20.30.

4. By beating them unjustly when there is no fault, 1 Sam. 20.33. or immoderately, unreasonably and basely, when there is a fault, doing it with bitterness without compassion, instruction, and prayer. These unnatural carriages exceedingly provoke Children to wrath, and thereby your Children are provoked by you to sin; for Children cannot bear cruel injuries from their very Parents, without being incited thereby to sinful anger. Therefore the Apostle saith, Provoke not your Children to anger: yet I say, Parents are not to withhold seasonable, necessary, and moderate correction from their Children, although the Children should be enraged and provoked to wrath by it; for Though they must not provoke them to wrath, yet they must not neglect to bring them up in the nurture and admonition of the Lord. They must not go from one extreme to another, i.e. from Rigidity to too much Lenity. Whiles Parents are cautioned against rigid severity. 'Tis necessary to guard them against too much indulgence, that they may not let their Children persevere in Vicious courses without control. Parents ought to take care of their Children's Souls, faithfully endeavoring to beat down sin in them by nurture or correction, and using all means possible to bring them up for Sons and Daughters to the Lord Almighty.

13. Whenever you reprove, instruct, whenever you find fault with any evil your Children have done, inform them of some good, that they should be doing. There are many that are apt to be much in reproving faults that are seldom or never teaching duties. The Wife thinks it her special privilege to check, and the Father's duty only to teach; yet when they are teaching them, Wives will quarrel with their Husbands for not giving better instructions to their Children; but will not allow their Husbands to speak to them in their presence, or they will find fault with the matter or

manner of instructing. Indeed while Children are young, the duty of teaching and instructing them is more incumbent on the Wife than the Husband; for while the Wife keeps in her place, and as she ought to be. Tit. 2.15. A keeper at home, she is most conversant with them, and hath most opportunities of conversing with them by way of Instruction, the good Wife that Solomon mentions in Prov. 31.26. *She opened her mouth with wisdom, and in her tongue is the law of kindness. She looketh well to the ways of her household.*

Those are far from having a law of kindness in their tongues, who are still casting forth in their Expressions the filth of their froward minds, and that Wife is far from carrying herself as a Christian Parent that is always raging against pretended faults, but never giving loving instructions or good advice or counsel. Parents ought to be giving pious instructions to their Children, when there is no cause of reproof, they ought to instruct every day, but reprove them only when an offense is committed. Instruction is seasonable when there is no need of reproof; but reproof is never profitable without instruction. When a fault is reproved, the evil of it must be shown to the Child offending, and the necessity if desisting, and the danger of continuing such a practice must be demonstrated, and how the Child ought to behave himself in his carriage towards God and them must be demonstrated. If Husband and Wife were faithful in this respect, there would not be such jarrings and contentions between them as there are.

14. Before you instruct or correct Children or Servants, beg God to direct you how to manage your instructions and corrections, and to sanctify them to their benefit, you cannot expect God to succeed that; which you do not beg God to bless. Instructions are so often given without success, because so often given without Prayer, and your Corrections are so often given in pas-

sion, that they are seldom given with moderation, and the gratifying of passion is oftener the ground of Correction then Reformation, because angry superiors will not allow themselves time to pray before they do correct. So that is made an act of rashness, which should be an act of seriousness. You complain of your inferiors' stubbornness, Children and Servants are stubborn, your instruction and correction doth influence them very little, but when did you make a solemn work by solemn, or ejaculatory Prayer, before you entered upon it? Blame your neglects of duty to God, as the ground of your inferiors' neglect of duty to you.

Lastly, If Wives would live in peace and amity with their Husbands, if any of them are married to a man that had Children by a former Wife, let such a Wife beware that she do not vilify her Children-in-law, nor represent every Childish act as an Abomination, when she cannot evidence them to be positively sinful. Some Wives will exclaim against their Children-in-law for very trifles, accuse them to their Husbands as guilty of stubbornness and rudeness to incense their Husbands against them, and if they cannot influence their Husbands to be dogged to them or if their Husbands will not countenance, and encourage their harsh dealings with them, they contend with their Husbands and will not permit them to enjoy any quiet in their Families. I say if such Wives cannot by any of their subtle contrivances and unjust complaints prevail with their Husbands to withdraw their affections from them, they will withdraw their affections from their Husbands and refuse to give them any conjugal respect. They approve of no Servants but such as will make complaints against their Children-in-law, and concur with them in vilifying of them, and such a course hath been the cause much discord between Husbands and Wives. Indeed it is a Mother-in-law's prudence to wink at many Childish faults in her Husband's Children by a former

Wife, and not aggravate every failing in them. Let Mothers-in-law know that they cannot justly claim a right to exercise equal Authority over them as over Children born of their own bodies, because not so nearly related to them, yea not related to them at all by blood, and notwithstanding what some Mother-in-laws have asserted, yet it cannot be thought true; that they are so much Mothers to their Children-in-law, as they are Wives to their Husbands: because their chiefest right of authority over their Children-in-law doth arise from their Husband's Resignation of them to their charge and Tutorage, and their own taking charge of them by virtue of the said Resignation.

  For the Mother-in-law's authority over the Children that are not born of her own body, is derived from her Husband, and conferred on her by her Husband, and as she hath not an equal authority over her own Children as her Husband hath, who is her superior by God's appointment, much less over her Children-in-law. 'Tis true as in the absence of the Husband, the Wife is principally concerned in the Government of the Family, and Children-in-law are Members of the Family, in that respect the Mother-in-law hath the same authority over them, as other Members of the Family. Therefore let all Mother-in-laws consider Doctor Harris, his last advice to his Wife. If you marry again, remember your own observation, that second Husbands are very uxorious, second Wives very prevalent, and therefore take heed that you do no ill office in estranging your Husband from his natural Children, and kindred; you shall thereby draw upon him a great sin, and judgment, if you kill in him natural affections. Wherefore if Mothers-in-law are so Resolute, and the fury of their Spirits is so raised, that they will exercise more authority over their Children-in-law, than their Husbands are willing to allow them; to preserve the peace of the Family, it is the Husband's prudence to place his first Wife's Children in other Families, where they may be piously educated, and that Wife hath no regard to the glory of God nor the honor of Religion that will oppose it, if the Husband be able to maintain them in other Families. The Apostle presseth all to *follow after the things that make for peace.* Rom. 14.19. This Exhortation doth concern the peace of Families as well as the peace of the Church, therefore whatever doth necessarily tend to preserve peace between such near Relations as Husband and Wife must be carefully followed, and whatever tends to beget strife and contention between them must be carefully avoided; for such froward Persons, as are promoters of discord, God hates. Prov. 6.19. Prov. 8.13. Therefore observe these following cautions.

First, Beware of being discontented with the condition or relation in which God hath placed you, for nothing doth more aim the Glory of God, more destroy and eat out your Comforts than discontent.

2. Beware of looking on one another with a disdainful eye, as if each of you did conceive yourself to excel, and were superior in worth to the other, for by having one another in contempt, you can never live peaceably together.

3. Beware of neglecting acts of conjugal love for that will breed strangeness between you. By this means such as heretofore lay in one another's bosoms, are grown so strange, that they cannot stay with content in one another's sight they will scarce look upon one another; who not long since professed dearly to love one another. 'Tis sad, yea very sad, that they who should be ready to die for one another, can hardly live with one another! Oh when will the love of many such Relations which hath waxen cold, gather heat again? Were it not monstrous that one Member of the body should withdraw offices of love from another, or should be as a stranger to it? So it is strange that Husband and Wife should

suspend the exercises of love to each other, that are as nearly allied as one Member of the body to another, these unnatural distances between Husbands and Wives are too open to be hid or denied. And is it not a reproach to Christianity, that such as are one flesh, should act as if they were not Members of the same World? If then you would live peaceably together, beware of suspending Acts of Love to each other.

4. Beware you do not reproach one another, for reproaches do make breaches, if one Friend do reproach another, there will be a breach of their Friendship, for bitter and calumniating words do very much vex our spirits, and usually the chiefest causes of discord between you. Wherefore I pray consider that Husbands and Wives continuing in strangeness to each other makes them at last become guilty of burnings and bitterness of spirit one against another, it will not only cause them to forbear the manifestations of kindness to each other, but to be cruel, and devise evil one against another. Therefore let me persuade you to love each other with a love of complacency. Let your delight be set on each other, and let all the lines of your affections be centered in each other. i.e. Let not every trifling occasion quench the flames of your affection, but let the heat and height of your love be placed upon one another, beyond your Children and other Friends. When such Relations decline in their love, they incline to hatred. Conjugal love being ill digested, or corrupted, turns to the greatest enmity. Husbands and Wives are under the closest obligations to love. Now, the closer any obligation is, the wider is the breach when once the obligation is broken or misimproved. If the Wife, whom the Husband dearly loved, begins to fall from him, or forsake his bed, she usually falls out with him. There hath been sad experience of this, and 'tis an argument where it happens, that such Wives did never love their Husbands upon Gospel-principles, or

in obedience to God's command, for as they who turn against the Truths of God, never received them in love, so she never in reality embraced her Husband in love, who turns against him: for when grace is the cement of affections, nothing can divide them. Certainly if Husbands and Wives would faithfully endeavor to observe the directions that I have given them concerning their carriages to each other, and to their Children and Servants, they would live more peaceably and comfortably together than they now do. 'Tis their unfaithfulness in relational duties that occasions much of their Discord. You Wives that pretend reasons for your contendings with your Husbands, and for your angry insulting language, endeavour to inform yourselves more fully of the nature of your relational duties, how you ought to carry it towards your Husbands, and to your Children and Servants, and endeavor a faithful discharge of those duties, and you will quickly find a better agreement between you. Thus I have ended what I have to say on this subject.

FINIS

www.ingramcontent.com/pod-product-compliance
Lightning Source LLC
Chambersburg PA
CBHW022116040426
42450CB00006B/721